a guide to

THRIVING

surviving

with mental illness

• • •

MEQUELL W. BUCK

ISBN: 1511450533
ISBN 13: 9781511450539

DEDICATION

to Adam, Max, Sam and Ella
who are the very best parts of my life.
I love you more. Yes possible.

TABLE OF CONTENTS

Marriage

Conclusion

FOREWORD

• • •

THERE IS SOMETHING TO THE old saying, "I don't care how much
you know until I know how much you care." Why is that? Well,
my experience has taught me that people do not desire direction, instruction or judgment. Instead we crave connection and
understanding. The moment you begin to hope for something
better is usually the moment right after you finally feel a measure of validation. Mental illness is ubiquitous in our world. In
fact, it always has been. Unfortunately, we tend to be a private
and stubborn species when it comes to personal trials and challenges. Despite the many centuries we have walked the face of
this planet we still struggle to be open with our weaknesses and
imperfections. Thus, healthy connections to self and attach-
ments to others remain elusive for many. The only proven path
to connection has ever been the one wherein you risk being
seen and known by others without assurances on the front end
that you will be accepted or empathized with. On our own we
are rarely at our best. Together, families, tribes, clans, villages,
faiths and the like have produced the greatest feats in human

happiness and progress. Isolation has a poor track record of generating health and healing.

Mental illness has long been a companion to many people I have known both personally and professionally. Those who have experienced victories are they who have embarked on an adventure of honest self-exploration and open examination and have risked being vulnerable with others who they desired and hoped would be compassionate stewards of their stories. More specifically they have opened up to fellow travelers in their own quest for mental and emotional peace and together they have experienced the epiphany that their situation is quite hopeful. That something, many things in fact, can be done together to improve and thrive. These precious souls have learned they are not helpless, but rather, they are indeed capable of having power over their situation. When you courageously live in consultation with others you open the portals to demonstrating that you can indeed trust yourself to be resourceful, creative, confident, and happy by controlling what you can. Without question this challenge is extremely difficult. Nonetheless, you can still have control over your situation to change what you can and to accept what you can't.

In these pages Mequell takes you on an insider's journey from mental anguish and despair, to hope and relief. Her credibility stems from her own quest and path with mental illness in a world full of people's good intentions, yet strewn with their poor execution of empathy, compassion and direction. Mequell is my friend and she is a fine example of tenacity and perseverance in the face of seeming hopelessness. She has discovered the truth of a better way, a path less traveled but ready to be well-worn by modern day explorers who follow her map. She is a real person living a real life. She is happy. She is funny. She has adversity. She has loss. She has faith. She has joy. She is honest. She is a wife. She is a mother. She is a friend. She manages her mental illness and lives a full life...and so can you.

Mark Bell
Licensed Marriage and Family Therapist

PREFACE

• • •

I NEVER INTENDED TO WRITE a book. Really I was just trying to go through life minding my own business. The idea of sharing my deepest, darkest struggles with the entire world is a little intimidating. I know there will be some who judge or criticize and just don't get it. I realize I have to not care. I didn't write this book for people like that. I wrote this book for those in the trenches who fight this battle every day. I understand the heavy load. There is a way to help lift that load so you can get out from under that dark cloud and feel the sun again. It's taken years for me to learn how to manage mental illness. I am a master now at working with the cycles and knowing what to do.

Once I figured out the secrets and truly began to thrive, I had people who were struggling ask me for help. At first it was only a few and I was happy to share what I had learned. As time went on more and more people started to reach out to me. There were so many people asking and I felt like I was giving the same information over and over so I decided to write it down. When people would ask for help I would give them my very rudimentary outline of the things that I had learned. That's how the book was started. Even then I still didn't love the idea of publishing a book for everyone to see. If someone asked me for help personally I was very open and honest. I loved helping other people with this very hard thing. I felt like I was born to do this. But publishing all my personal struggles and announcing to the world that I have mental illness? No thanks. So I sat right where I was for two years sharing with anyone who asked but certainly not advertising. But I kept getting nudges. At first those nudges were small and easy to ignore but they kept getting louder. Finally the nudges were so loud I felt like someone was shaking me and yelling in my face: "Publish that book! Somebody needs you!" So if you are that someone who's been searching for help, this book is for you. I did it all for you.

CHAPTER 1

¿CUAL ES SU PROBLEMA?

• • •

So, you've got a problem and you don't know exactly what it is or why it started. All you know is something is wrong. Very wrong. Welcome to the club.

Recently I was having hair issues. As in I hated my hair. It didn't lay right, the shape was off and no matter how much time I spent on it, it never actually looked good. I tried talking to my hair dresser about it and even offered a few suggestions and brought in a pretty picture of lovely, flowing locks. It did not work. I still had bad hair. So one weekend when I was in Las Vegas where I used to live and happened to know of a great hair dresser, I made an appointment. I went in and sat down in the chair and the first thing he said was "Your hair has a lot of things wrong with it." He then went on to describe them all. I was so relieved he could see the problems I nearly jumped up and kissed him. I refrained since I'm married and it would have been awkward. Also my husband was in the next chair (yes, he went to the hair salon with me and got major brownie points for suffering through the experience and no, it's never happened before). The reason I was so happy was that I knew there were issues with my hair even though my current hair dresser said there weren't because she had fixed them. Just knowing that someone recognized them and knew what to do made me feel like I was in good hands and I wasn't crazy. I left that day with good hair and a renewed faith in the beauty industry.

Figuring out mental illness is much the same way. In the beginning all you know is that something is wrong. You feel off but you can't explain why. It's almost like you're living in a parallel universe and you feel like a shadow of your former self. Your emotions are out of control and way too intense producing crying spells or anxiety so powerful that it cripples you and leaves you curled up in the fetal position on your closet floor. They're not matching up to what's actually going on in your life and you don't understand why these emotions are overtaking your life. Everything feels overwhelming and hopeless like you're never going to feel better again. Your energy drops and basic things that were just a normal part of your day before (like showering and eating) now seem beyond what you are capable of doing on a daily basis. You can't get out of bed and sleep for hours each day. You dread waking up to this new reality. You can't pinpoint any one thing that's happened to start this train of events nor can you understand exactly why all this is happening. You don't know how to get everything to stop or how to feel good again. You just want your life back. You just want this to stop. I hear you. I understand your pain.

My goal in writing this is to be that helpful hairdresser. There are many things that you can do to successfully live with mental illness. I know what the challenges are. I know the weight it is trying to live your life. I know sometimes you just want to give up because it seems too much. I am here to coach you through the hard times and to tell you it won't always be this hard. I am here to give you ideas on concrete things that will improve your quality of life. I am here to help you see what areas you can become strong in with some focused effort. I am here to help you not just survive, but thrive while dealing with mental illness in whatever situation you find yourself in. It can be done. I am living proof. I'm here to help you work smarter, not harder and to find ways to work with mental illness instead of constantly fighting against it. It seems a little counterintuitive but pushing against that brick wall is exhausting and you're not going to push it over. Take a step back, roll up your sleeves and let's figure out how to have a peaceful coexistence with a very difficult foe. Although my diagnosis is bipolar disorder, there are many crossovers in the mental illness arena. I have experience with symptoms of major depression, of intense anxiety and of obsessive compulsive tendencies. The things that I have learned over my many years of living with this are invaluable to me and will help others with many types of mental illnesses. I recognize the challenges that come from living with mental illness and I know what to do. So sit back, relax and trust me that you are in good hands.

This book is designed to give you practical advice and steps to work on day to day to improve your quality of life.

It's designed to educate you from an insider's point of view on how to successfully maneuver the swings and challenges that come with mental illness. It's designed to make you strong in areas that are crushing you now. This is not an academic book. I am not a doctor and my intent is not to explain the chemical reactions in the brain with your medication or how the neurotransmitters work with brain wave communication. I'm not here to explain academic theories behind mental illness nor is this an authoritative treatise that sites studies done. This book is different. It's a how-to guide if you will. This book will teach you principles to manage mental illness so you can have a high quality of life and be happy for years to come even while living with mental illness. This will help you prioritize what's important for you and give you the tools and perspective to live your life according to your priorities while cutting out all the extras that weigh you down and can drown you when you have this heavy weight. If you follow these principles, you can keep your head above water. You can feel good and feel alive and live a purposeful and mean-ingful life. Mental illness does not have to be a death sen-tence. It does not have to be the end of your happiness. It does not have to crush you. You just have to work with it. You will become like a ninja gracefully ducking and spinning to avoid the heavy blows that come at you from every side when you're living with this. You will learn how to go on the attack and be proactive at fighting back so the blows won't come as fast and as hard. You will become a ninja master like Kung Fu Panda minus the dumplings. Prepare your minds. I've got your back.

I am an active member of the LDS Church[1] a.k.a. Mormon. I have a strong belief in God. Although this is not a religious book in nature, I do occasionally reference things that might require a few words of explanation. I have included brief footnotes to explain specific terminology so you know what the heck I'm talking about. I grew up in the church and it's always been an important part of my life. I have been married for eighteen years to my husband Adam and have three fantastic teenage kids Max, Sam and Ella who make me laugh every day. Let me back up a little bit here. I, Mequell, having been born of goodly parents... Seriously. My parents are great. In fact my patriarchal blessing[2] tells me that they were picked out specifically for me so that I could receive the proper training. They trained me in all sorts of ways. They trained me to work hard. They trained me to set goals. They trained me to be dedicated in my service to the Lord. They trained me to have a positive attitude. In my house growing up, can't was the other four letter word. Saying "can't" elicited a stronger response from my dad than any cuss word I could have said. (Alright, he grew up on a ranch in Idaho where there are different language standards so some four letter words that might be cuss words to you, may not be to him. Thought you'd want to know.) Honestly though, can't was a bad, bad word. We had to pay twenty-five cents into a jar every time we said the word "can't." I remember many lessons both as a family and one-on-one with my dad where we went over what my goals were in dif-

---

1   The Church of Jesus Christ of Latter-Day Saints
2   A special, personal blessing given once in a lifetime to a person that is intended to guide and direct them in making choices for their lives.

ferent areas of my life. He always had (and still does) a yellow legal pad with goals written on them for every aspect of his life. He and my mom were great examples in that area. They were so intent on us learning to think like champions that *Winners & Losers* by Sydney J. Harris was required reading in our house.

One summer when I was in elementary school, my parents came to my two oldest brothers and I with a proposal. They had purchased some poker chips which we called COW chips. It stood for "Currency of Winners." They had a list of things for us to work on and we would earn COW chips for each task accomplished. At the end of the summer, whoever had the most COW chips would get $50.00, second place would get $40.00 and third place would get $25.00. We earned COW chips by working around the house, having a good attitude about things, and reading Value Tale books. This was a set of books that taught about different values. For example *The Value of Believing in Yourself: The Story of Louis Pasteur*. The books were about sixty pages long and took an hour or so to read. Every chore earned a different amount of COW chips depending on how long it took and how dreaded the task was (like weeding, ugh, which garnered three chips I think). We would lose chips by fighting with each other or saying the bad can't word. My mom has told me that this was the best summer of our childhood. Amazing how motivated we were when money was involved. As the summer drew to a close and the deadline for earning COW chips came near, there was a mad rush to acquire more. My older brother Jody and I were neck and neck. The cut-off was Sunday at 5:00 pm. After church, he was assigned to do the dishes which would earn him a few chips. I had an hour which would give me enough time to read one more value book which was worth five chips. I was going to win! Jody came to talk with me and asked me not to read the book. If I didn't, we would tie. Jody and I were good friends. He was always nice to me even when his friends were around. I decided that I wouldn't read the book. We shared first place and earned $45.00 apiece and I came away feeling so lucky to have such a great big brother.

We had good feelings and good relationships in our home growing up. There was also a lot of laughter. Our last name was Williams so I remember sitting at the dinner table and my dad would chant "What's our favorite letter?" and we would all yell "W!" It was a stretch for me to take on a different last name when I got married because I felt very loyal to my family and our name. I have three brothers which was fantastic in so many ways, mainly because I got to watch sports whenever I wanted to! And I knew all the rules so I could keep up in any of them. This has served me well in my life. After I graduated from college and started working at an ad agency, I won the football pool in the office for the season and won lots of money which totally rocked. It also made me feel a bit smug when the good ol' boys club was taken down a notch by the girl from the Research Department who everyone thought were nerds. (I'm a tad bit competitive.)

It is also a lot of fun to watch with my husband Adam who is a basketball fan. March Madness is my favorite time of year. We fill out the brackets and have a friendly wager for whoever wins like the time after my son was born and the loser had to change his diapers for a whole week. Fortunately I know the tricks like picking the number 12 seed upsets over the number 5 teams. It happens every March Madness. Yep, I got good training in my home.

When I was in third grade, my parents sat all of us kids down at the table and asked us to make a list of the things we wanted to do for after school activities. My list had about twenty things on it. It had everything from gymnastics, ice skating, piano to girl scouts and 4-H club. My parents said I had to pick just one which was excruciating. How could I possibly decide? I wanted to do everything. After deliberation, we decided that I could start gymnastics which began a fifteen year affair with the sport. I loved gymnastics. I worked my way quickly through the recreational program and started on the competitive team along with my brothers. We spent hours at the gym. It quickly became my whole life outside of school. I went every day and by the time I was in high school, I trained for twenty-four hours each week. Even when I had spare time I wanted to go to the gym. My mom made a deal with me. She would let me go to open gym hours in addition to my regular training if I would spend one hour on the beam each time I went. Drat. She must have had me pegged because the only reason I wanted to go was to jump on the trampoline and tumble into the pit (which is a big hole in the ground filled with foam cubes so you can learn new tricks). She drove a hard bargain and in the end, I agreed. All that beam time paid off when I was fourteen. I won first place in the Western Regionals

(Western U.S.) on beam and fourth in the All-Around. I was driven, motivated and didn't see anything that could stop me.

Along with success in the gym, I also had success academically. When I was in sixth grade I was chosen to be part of the gifted program. I realize today we refer to every child as "gifted" but back then we weren't so politically correct. I like to think I truly was one of the rare exceptions. There was one class in the district so I was bussed to a separate school. When I was in junior high school I took advanced math classes over at the high school for the first hour of the day. School came very easily to me, especially math and I always got A's. I put a lot of time and energy into studying because it was important to me to do my best all the time.

Even though I was quiet and well behaved in school, I had a mischievous streak. My sophomore year, we had block days. On my "A" day classes, I had second lunch but all of my friends had first lunch. One day after class, I stayed behind and told my Social Studies teacher that I had a problem. It was very embarrassing to me so I asked him not to say anything to anyone about it, even my parents. (Are you suspicious already? If I were him I would have been.) Anyway, I told him I had a bladder control problem and that I would occasionally have to get up from class to go to the bathroom. I just wanted him to know ahead of time so I wouldn't have to embarrass myself by asking every time I needed to leave. After that, I would spontaneously get up in the middle of class and go meet my friends for lunch. Because I was such a good student and so well behaved, no one ever suspected or found out until I was laughing about it a few years ago as an adult. My mom was shocked! She couldn't believe I would ever do such a thing!

At the end of my sophomore year of high school we moved to California. It was a sad move for me because we moved away from all of my cousins and extended family and my gym. There was not a good gymnastics program near our new house. I had been having issues with injuries and shin splints so I made the decision to stop gymnastics and become more involved at school. I tried out for cheerleading and made the Varsity Squad on account of my superior tumbling skills. I also tried out for the volleyball team and in the spring, the track team. I ran the hurdles and placed in state my first year of running. I also broke twenty year old school records for the fastest time in the 110 meter hurdles and the 330 meter hurdles. I continued to do well in school taking college courses while still in high school and graduating 11th in my class.

While I was in high school, cheerleading and participating in sports, I also worked three jobs. At nights I worked at The Old Spaghetti Factory bussing tables and being a hostess. On the weekends I worked at Blockbuster and Saturday mornings I did housecleaning for a neighbor lady. One time someone at work asked me why I had so many jobs and I told him I was saving money. He asked what I was saving for. A car? Christmas? I told him I was saving just to save. I was always very conservative and responsible with my money. By the time I started college at BYU, I had enough to pay for my first year of school without working during the school year. I missed gymnastics and thought I would take a recreational class just for fun. The first week of classes, the teacher called in the head gymnastics coach for BYU and told him he needed to see something. He came in and watched one of our classes and even though a few years had gone by, I still was able to do a lot of the same tricks and was a strong tumbler. I ended up walking on the gymnastics team and worked hard to earn a spot to compete for them. I was excited for my first meet. On my first event, floor exercise, I fell during my last tumbling pass and injured my knee. I ended up needing surgery and this officially became the end of my gymnastics career.

It was very difficult for me to not have something I excelled in. I felt average when I didn't have something to pour my heart, time and effort into. I didn't like feeling average. I wondered how I was special? What made me unique? What made me an exceptional person if I didn't have some measure or some achievement to gauge it by? This turned out to be the first step in a very long (and might I add painful) life lesson for me. Heavenly Father does not look at our goals and accomplishments to determine whether or not we are exceptional people and worthy of his kingdom. In fact, those things actually matter very little to him. His number one concern is our personal development. Who are we becoming? Sometimes having goals and achievements help us to develop personally and become a better person. They can help us learn to work hard, to overcome challenges, to focus and learn discipline. But just because we achieve high goals and excel does not necessarily mean we have become a better person along the way. Although achieving high goals can make us better, it can also have the opposite effect and we can begin to think that our value lies in achievements, not our character. For me, because so many things had come easier to me, I didn't understand those who struggled in areas that I excelled in. I thought that if they would just apply themselves and work hard, they too could achieve the same measure of success. I hate to say it, but I was a little bit judgy. Oh I wouldn't say it out loud to other people because that would be mean but I thought it in my head. I didn't have compassion for others because I thought they were struggling because they didn't work hard or didn't want it bad enough or because they had a negative thought process and didn't believe they could do it. Not to say I wasn't kind to people because I did try to be. I just didn't understand at all. I totally didn't get it.

As a side note here let me just say never be judgy. Heavenly Father has a wonderful way of teaching things that we just don't get. In my opinion, it's always better to try to understand without being compelled because being compelled is always painful. This end though to my gymnastics career turned out to be a wonderful learning opportunity for me. It took gymnastics out of the number one priority spot in my life and opened the way for me to fill it with God. I relied on him to learn and grow and my testimony did. I came to understand that I was valuable to him even without all the accolades to prove my worth. I learned this lesson at level one. Maaaaybe level two if I'm being generous to myself. But at least this lesson was now on my radar and I could work on it on my own without all the previously mentioned painful compelling.

So back to my story. Gymnastics was now over and because I hadn't worked, I was out of money. I moved back home and enrolled at the local junior college to continue my education and also got a job. I joined the track team because honestly a life without sports (even though it wasn't my TOP top priority anymore) was still a sad life for me to live. I finished my Associate's Degree that year and also placed in the state championship meet in my hurdle events. I felt like I was back on top of my game. I also started thinking more seriously about serving a mission[3].

I had always wanted to serve from the time I was very young. When I was little, I wanted to marry my big brother Jody when I grew up. He was awesome. He was so cute and nice and I thought he would make a wonderful husband. Well I soon found out that you can't marry your brother so I decided I would marry my cousin Rick who was almost as cute and almost as nice. When I received the crushing blow that you can't marry your cousin either, I decided I wouldn't get married at all and instead I would go on a mission. Back then I thought you chose one or the other and since I couldn't marry anyone I wanted to, I decided I would pick a mission. My reasons for wanting to serve may have been a little off but nevertheless, the desire was there. That desire stayed with me all the way through my growing up years even when I realized it wasn't an either/or situation. So now I had the opportunity to make that

---

3   A mission is a voluntary opportunity to proselyte and teach other people about the church.

choice for real. I submitted my papers and was called to serve in the Utah Salt Lake City Mission.

I spent the first year pushing and pushing and pushing to keep the rules exactly and to reach the high goals of teaching and baptizing. I have to say I didn't enjoy it as much as I could have but I worked very hard. About a year in is when everything started crumbling down for me. I couldn't sleep at night because I was so worried and anxious and my mind would race about all the things I needed to do. I would be up for two or three days at a time. I also had a hard time eating. Nothing tasted good. It's a good thing that I served a mission in Salt Lake where we had wonderful members that would feed us every night. I would always eat at least an acceptable amount because it would be rude not to but the fact was I just wasn't hungry. I felt completely overwhelmed and inadequate. I was emotional in all the wrong ways. I couldn't keep up. My energy level dropped drastically. I felt like a failure because I didn't understand what was happening. I started seeing a counselor to try and help me handle the pressures and anxieties I was feeling.

Fortunately I had an amazing mission president. He called me in and talked to me. He asked me if I had any idea how much the Lord loved me. He also took away all of the mission rules. He actually said to me, "Sister Williams, you have no rules." He told me to get up when I felt like it. He said if I wanted to go shopping in the middle of the day, go shopping. He told me I didn't have any requirements for teaching or tracting. He even told me I could call home if I wanted to. Looking back I can't believe that he did that. I think that any other mission president would have sent me home. That would have completely crushed me further confirming that I would never measure up. Instead he expressed his confidence in me and told me that my offering was enough.

Thinking back to my mission president though, I know the only reason he was able to take away the rules and all the pressures that went along with them was because he knew 100% I wouldn't abuse that. He knew I would still study my scriptures. He knew I would still bear testimony and find and teach investigators. He knew I would still pray with my companion and work hard. He knew he could count on me to be obedient to gospel principles. He knew me. All he did when he removed the rules was take away the pressure and help me to feel that what I could do was enough.

This lesson, that my best is good enough, has taken a long time in learning. My wonderful mission president did his best to help me understand that the Lord does not expect more than I have to offer. After he took away the rules I did feel immediate relief. I was able to spend time sifting through in my mind what the Lord wanted me to do and what was ok to let go of. I knew he wanted me to teach and bear testimony. I knew he wanted me to study and grow spiritually. I knew he wanted me to obey gospel principles and I did. My companion through this was perfect for me. She had a strong testimony but also had the ability to lighten up and really have fun. She made it easy for me to take a break when I needed to and make sure I didn't push to the point of exhaustion. There was a day when my companion and I spent the afternoon driving in the mountains after a morning zone conference. There was a day when we stopped at Ross and bought a swim suit then sat in the hot tub in the women's locker room of the old Deseret Gym. But there were many more days that we spent studying together and finding and teaching investigators. Our teaching pool was full and I had never had as many baptisms as I did during that time period. We were serving on the University of Utah campus and the energy with the students was invigorating. We worked together with them and spent much time at the Institute[4] working in collaboration.

This was the point when I started to love being a missionary. I connected with my investigators on a very different level. I got to know them more as people instead of just teaching opportunities. My companion and I even called them "our people" meaning they felt like friends we had always known. All of the people I have kept in touch with after my mission were ones that I met and taught after this point. All I had to do was love them and I did.

This shift in attitude for me lasted about four months. Then I was transferred to another area with a different companion. She was a wonderful missionary and very obedient. I felt like I had been doing so well and I didn't want to let her down by not following the rules with exactness. As much as the mission president could do to ease the expectations for me, it was still a mission and in my mind success was still measured by finding and teaching opportunities, hours worked,

---

4 Religious instruction building on a college campus

and baptisms. Toward the end of that first month we had together, our mission baptism goal did not look like it would be reached. The assistants to the president selected a handful of companionships to commit to finding and teaching a few more people by the end of the month. My companion and I were on the short list.

We busted our butts. (Am I allowed to say that?) We tracked and followed up with every member and every lead we could get. We worked from sun up to sun down pounding the pavement. And we were victorious! We found and taught two more people in that last week for our mission to reach their goal. They also happened to get baptized. I was so proud but it came at a cost for me. I was slipping right back in the same position I'd been in earlier. I couldn't sleep. I had very little energy and no appetite. I continued to push to keep all of the rules and work as hard as I could but it wasn't working.

My companion was transferred and I was given a new missionary to train. This just increased the pressure for me to try and be perfect to teach her how to be a great missionary. This is when the bottom completely fell out. It was about six more weeks until my eighteen months was up and it would be time to go home. I knew I couldn't make it. I didn't have six more weeks in me. I didn't even have one more day in me. I was done. Stick a fork in me and roll me over. It was very late at night and my companion was sleeping. I was just thinking about how to make the pressure stop. I knew I would never measure up. I knew I would never be enough. I knew I wasn't going to make it. I opened up the cabinet and saw five or six bottles of pills. Some were old prescriptions from previous missionaries. Some were vitamins and herbal supplements. I got a big glass of water and sat down. I slowly and methodically swallowed every single pill. It was probably over one hundred. I laid down and cried. After a few minutes I thought about what I had done and I knew that I did not want to die. I called my zone leader who came and picked my companion and I up and we drove to the emergency room.

I met with a psychiatrist and he concluded that I had Obsessive-Compulsive disorder. You know, because I was so freaky about following the rules with exactness. I distinctly remember one time racing across the room and leaping in to bed right as the clock was turning 10:31 I was devastated and spent the next half hour languishing with guilt that comes from breaking the rule of a 10:30 bedtime. I laugh now because it seems so absurd but that's because now I'm thinking clearly. Turns out I don't have OCD I'm just a perfectionist which is a whole other problem in and of itself.

This is when my learning curve started. I started at zero. I knew nothing of what a diagnosis of mental illness would mean to me or things I could do to feel better. I had no reference point. I didn't know anyone with a diagnosis of mental illness. I didn't know what questions to ask. I didn't even know how much I didn't know. If I knew then what I know now, I could have saved myself years and years of pain, frustration and feelings of hopelessness and feeling out of control. This is what I'm trying to help you avoid. If you get all the tools now, your learning curve won't be counted in years, it will be counted in months or even weeks. That is the greatest gift I can give you. This is what I wish someone had given me.

When I was first diagnosed, I had no idea what to expect. I knew this was affecting my life tremendously. I was in a complete tailspin. I didn't know which way was up and I didn't have anywhere to turn for answers. I was confused about a mental illness diagnosis. I had no understanding of what it was or what it would mean for my life but I was certain that it was the worst thing that had ever happened to me. I felt like I was broken in so many ways. What I didn't realize is dealing with mental illness would be a huge blessing for me and it has been. It's been a blessing to my marriage and a blessing to my family. I am a stronger, kinder, more understanding person because of it. My husband and kids are better people because of it. They are able to get outside themselves and be aware of things they can do to make a difference in the lives of other people. The things that I have learned and the person I've become is so much better than I would have been otherwise. Yes it's hard. Yes I sometimes wish I didn't have to deal with it. But if I got to choose my own trial in life, I would choose this (okay maybe only eight out of ten times but still). I would choose this because the end result, the life I have now that's full of purpose and wisdom and meaning, I would never give up for anything. I wouldn't have this life and this perspective without mental illness. I'm happy and excited about my life and alive in every sense of the word. I live out loud and on purpose. As my son likes to say YOLO. You Only Live Once. Don't despair. Your one life can still be amazing.

The key to having a life like this with mental illness is focusing on solutions and things you can control. In our family mission statement, one of the lines is this: "We focus on solutions instead of problems." There are many solutions and things that you can do to alleviate the tremendous weight and burdens that come from living with mental illness. Focus on the things that you can do to make it better and understand that you can still have control over your life. By focusing on the small things that you can control, you will be able to handle the big things that come from mental illness better. They won't crush you. You'll be stronger and more equipped with a greater understanding of what's happening with your illness. You'll be able to see your situation from an intellectual point of view instead of getting caught up and thrown around by the overwhelming emotions. By doing this, you can ride the wave over the vortex instead of getting sucked inside. It helps you keep the proper perspective and helps you not to panic when the hard times come. It will make you realize these hard times are temporary and you can get through them. This isn't an easy thing to learn. It takes practice. A lot of practice. But you get better with each round until you're so good at riding over the vortex, your heart rate barely accelerates. But let's not get ahead of ourselves because in the beginning, not gonna lie, it's rough.

First, there are some key things I want you to understand. This is what I wish someone would have told me in the beginning:

1. It can take a really long time to figure out what the problem actually is but don't worry, each step brings you closer to finding it.

2. Once you know what the problem is, finding the right medication can also take a really long time and you will probably have to cycle through a number of different ones before you find the combination that works best for you.

3. Medication is not the entire solution. It's *part* of the solution and absolutely essential (we'll talk more about this later) but there is a lot of work that you will need to do in addition to it.

4. You are not broken, inferior or subpar because you have a mental illness. It's just a problem that you deal with. It actually is temporary when you consider eternity.

5. Your life is not relegated to merely existing. In the beginning it takes a herculean effort just to get through the day but it gets better and you can be happy, productive and successful in your life.

6. It does not go away and you won't be cured but you can learn to manage it so well that it almost won't matter that you have it. Almost.

The fact is, mental illness is loaded with misinformation and carries a really bad rap. After all, who wants to be "crazy"? There is not the same kind of open support that comes from dealing with other physical illnesses like cancer or diabetes.

My friend Melody was diagnosed with cancer. Our other friend Rachel, who had been diagnosed a few years earlier with the same type of cancer knew exactly what to do. They went out to dinner with their husbands and discussed what they could expect. They talked about treatment plans and how Melody would feel and what kind of support she would need from her husband. Rachel also talked to our other friends and told us what kind of things would be needed and how we could help (like putting together a chemo bag that was a big, fun purse filled with books and magazines and treats). Rachel threw her a support party where everyone showed up and gave gifts that would help Melody during the treatments. Melody even got to show off her wig (which by the way, looked remarkably similar to my hair after it was good again).

I have to admit I was a little bit jealous. I would have LOVED someone to take me under their wing and explain how I was going to feel, what was going to happen and know all the things that would help. And really, I wanted a party! How amazing would it have been to have a group of people together cheering for me and who I knew I could call on during difficult times? Then I thought about it. In order for that to happen, I would actually have to tell everyone I have bipolar and frankly, I'm a little bit chicken about announcing it to the world (although if you're reading this, I think my cover is blown). I do have a handful of friends who know I have bipolar but this is not something I generally tell people right away. I feel that if people get to know me first and then later find out I have mental illness (after they've already formed an opinion of me) it's different than that being the first thing they know about me. I feel like I get a better chance to make friends and people get a more accurate picture of who I am instead of them having a preconceived notion about someone with mental illness because let's be honest here, it happens. Sometimes I am embarrassed and wish I had a more "acceptable" illness or at least one that is better understood. I watched my friend through the cancer drive where everyone was buying t-shirts and hats to support the cause and I wanted a t-shirt too. BIPOLAR SURVIVOR! But really would I wear it? Uh, no. Can you imagine the looks I would get? I have a t-shirt that says "I HEART ME" on it and I get enough weird looks when I wear that. I don't think I've got the nerve to wear a bipolar survivor shirt.

I am here for you to be that supportive friend. I know the journey up ahead of you and it's going to be tough. But I also know that you can do it. This is something that you can come out of on the other side stronger, wiser and more improved. So go grab a party hat and some horn blowers and let's get this party started!

CHAPTER 2

THE "D" WORD

• • •

CALM DOWN, I'M TALKING ABOUT diagnosis. It's just like in the twelve steps. The first step is recognizing you have a problem. After that, you find out how to fix it. You are dealing with a big, fat, hairy problem and you won't be able to fix it on your own.

There's not a lot of understanding from anyone when it comes to mental illness from either the person being diagnosed or those around them. This can make sharing this information with others difficult. I have a love/hate relationship with being open about my bipolar diagnosis. I love when I can help other people or connect with someone I otherwise wouldn't have. I hate having people who don't understand or get it know this very personal, challenging thing in my life. Understanding more about mental illness and that I am not my symptoms helped me feel much better about being open and sharing. Always when I tell people that I have bipolar I get the same response: "You?! You're kidding! I would NEVER have guessed!" You just don't know what people are dealing with behind closed doors so give them the benefit of the doubt and treat them kindly and without judgment.

Chances are that if you're reading this, you already know you're dealing with mental illness. It may be onset by a temporary situation such as loss of a loved one, post baby blues or something similar. Regardless, I probably don't have to describe the symptoms to you because you already know. But just in case it's a family member who has picked this up or the jury's still out on exactly what your problem is, we'll chat about this anyway.

Depression is the most common form of mental illness. I'm not talking depression with a little "d." I'm not talking about feeling sad about your favorite show being cancelled or even sad about your best friend moving across the country. I'm not talking about feeling bummed out or having an off day. I'm talking about not being able to get out of bed in the morning. I'm talking about sleeping and/or crying for hours on end. (Or maybe you're a multi-tasker and you cry while you sleep just to be more efficient.) I'm talking about breaking down while trying to perform the simple tasks of going about everyday life. I'm talking about the frozen smile you put on your face when you go out in public and hope to high heaven that no one looks too close or hugs you or something crazy like that are because you're going to lose it and weep uncontrollably and not be able to explain why. I'm talking about losing all interest in things that you normally love. I'm talking about withdrawing from everyone and everything that previously held your interest because it's too overwhelming and you just can't do it.

I'm talking about emotions so fragile that one minute you're calmly doing the dishes and the next you're sobbing into the dishcloth or even worse, rage is shooting through you so violently that you want to throw the dishes at the wall. I'm talking about DEPRESSION with a big, fat" D!" I hear you. I have felt these emotions.

Back before I was stable, when I was in meltdown mode as I liked to call it, I usually ended up in a puddle on the floor. I'm not sure when it started or why the floor seemed to beckon me, but down I went right then and right there. It was usually in the kitchen since that's where I spent a lot of my time in the evenings when the meltdowns happened. My kids were pretty conditioned when this happened (used to happen a lot so we had to get a routine you see). Sam or Ella would run to get a small pillow off the couch and a blanket from the basket in the family room and I would go into my special yoga pose that's supposed to lighten the heart and bring happiness. It had to be the small couch pillow because a regular pillow would put my head too high for the pose. I would lay flat on my back (on my hardwood floor) perfectly straight with my legs together looking straight up at the ceiling. I would spread my arms straight out with my palms up so I looked like a 'T' on the ground. One of them would put the pillow under my head while the other would spread the blanket over the top of me. Then they would both pick a side and lay down next to me with an arm over me hugging me on the ground and we waited it out.

Usually mental illness comes in a party pack meaning you don't just get one simple thing to deal with, you get an entire package of different symptoms that make getting an actual accurate diagnosis extremely difficult. Depression can be accompanied by some serious anxiety. Sometimes it's social anxiety that makes it difficult for you to go out in public and interact with people. Even something as simple as picking up your child from school can bring on a full blown panic attack with your heart racing so fast you can't make yourself get out the door. Sometimes even something as simple as having anyone over to your home makes you so anxious you find yourself dodging phone calls and eye to eye contact with people so they won't ask and you won't have to be put in the awkward situation of stammering through some fabricated excuse just to get out of it.

If you are living with someone and trying to understand why this is happening, remember they are probably just as confused as you are. They don't know what's going on. They don't know why it's happening. They don't know how to make it stop. Be aware though that this is very real. Do NOT under any circumstances tell them to suck it up or tell them to think happy thoughts and get over it. Even worse, do not ask them if they've tried to pray or read their scriptures. Do not tell them to just get outside themselves and serve. They are in survival mode. If you tell them this, you are not helping the situation. In fact you are making it much worse. Don't you think they've already tried to suck it up? Don't you think they've already tried thinking happy thoughts? Don't you realize that by asking if they've prayed or read their scriptures you're implying that their illness is a spiritual inadequacy?

You're basically telling them that if they had a stronger testimony they wouldn't be struggling. How much can I reiterate this ... NOT helpful! And also NOT true! Now I don't want to discount these things because they are important and they can help but thinking that they will solve the crushing weight of mental illness is a little naïve and uneducated.

In the beginning I thought mental illness was a weakness that if I was just strong and determined enough, I could overcome. I had always learned about persistence and the power of positive thinking and believed this should be able to fix my problem. It didn't. It just made me feel worse that I was not strong enough to do it. I have since changed my tune. It's come through understanding what mental illness is and what it isn't. It is a real, physical challenge that requires physical treatment to help. It is not a deficiency in character, a spiritual inadequacy or any weakness on your part.

Once I understood the difference, I was freed from so much guilt. Just like a cancer patient would never think receiving chemotherapy treatments was a sign of weakness, we also should not think receiving treatment for mental illness is a sign of weakness. Oddly enough, I would rather know I have a mental illness than to just think the problem is my shortcoming. For instance, I realize I'm still in my pajamas at 6:30 pm and I'm sobbing on the floor with spatula in hand while dinner is cooking on the stove and I can't form a coherent response as to why but it's not because I'm a mess, it's because I'm in a down cycle with bipolar and it will be better tomorrow. It's a wonderfully freeing thing to separate myself from the symptoms.

This is a common mistake that people make. Or, I realize that yesterday I got up early and went on a bike ride then did some laundry and detailed my car all while taking care of my three kids under five and before my 2:00 pm doctors' appointment but that is because I was manic and that level of activity should not be used as an everyday standard for productivity. Again, I am not my symptoms. I just have to be aware enough of them to separate myself intellectually from the emotions I'm feeling.

It's also important to be aware of how you feel when you're up. Are you still sleeping (a full eight hours, three or four doesn't count)? Do you feel peaceful, calm and happy or are you agitated and frustrated with the people around you because they are moving waaaay too slow? When I'm manic, it probably looks amusing from the outside. Because I chart (again, we'll talk more about this later) I know when I am manic and I plan my life accordingly. I get things done fast. I mean really fast. I can do a major two week shopping trip for the family at Wal-mart and be in and out in forty minutes. We're talking Wal-mart where the lines are at least twenty minutes long. I have my grocery list organized into store sections and I practically run through the store I'm going so fast. My husband has tried to accompany me on these trips and it doesn't work. He walks at normal-responsible-adult-person speed and keeps getting lost in the aisles. My teenage boys on the other hand are great to have along. They have no problem running through the aisles with a big ol' cart tipping on two wheels because they're taking the corners so fast. It's actually kind of fun to get so much done. I feel like a giant organizational whirlwind as I sprint through the house rotating laundry, menu planning, balancing accounts and running the monthly financial reports for our home all before 10:00 am. Just thinking about the mania makes me happy. (See, mental illness isn't entirely bad!) BUT (the big but) I also am very snappy with people because they are not moving fast enough for my liking. When I have conversations with people my brain jumps from topic to topic so fast that when they are responding to me I am already two topics ahead. I wonder "Why are we still talking about that? This part of the conversation is over. Keep up pal!" (envision me snapping my fingers quickly so they understand the pace they need to be at). If you feel like this sometimes, be aware that it isn't entirely normal. Other people around you are not dim-witted sloths, you are just manic. Try to be patient and keep your irritation under control as you realize the problem might be you.

I get asked the question sometimes "But how did you know you had bipolar?" The answer is I didn't. I didn't for a lot of years. I knew something was wrong but didn't know exactly what. I searched a long time in every avenue I could think of. Many people along the way were confident that they knew what was wrong and their treatment plan would eliminate my problem but nothing I tried helped enough to lift the weight for me to be able to breathe. All those treatment plans did help slightly but I needed some heavy lifting for me to be able to function and have a happy life. I just kept searching. It took a lot of time for me to put together all the pieces to figure out what the puzzle looked like. I kept trying to address only the low points. It took a lot of visits to doctors and counselors and a lot of awareness on my part to figure out what was relevant and come to the correct diagnosis. Have faith and be aware that this is a process. It takes time to figure out what is wrong. It takes time to figure out a treatment plan. It takes time to work through medication issues and counseling. Don't get frustrated with the process and don't give up because you think it's not working. Keep plodding slowly along and realize that improvement will take time. Be okay with that.

I love watching the Biggest Loser (with a pint of Häagen-Dazs ice cream by the way which is okay because I've already worked out for the day before the show started). One of the things the trainers constantly say is it took years for your body to become like this. It's not going to change overnight. But if you consistently apply the correct principles of exercise and proper nutrition, your body will change. You just have to be patient with it. Addressing mental illness is the same way. It's not going to be fixed overnight. There's not a magic pill that will make everything better. The right medication will help lift the burden tremendously and the work you do in figuring out how to handle stress, manage the swings and work to keep a healthy perspective will manage the rest. But it takes time to get good at all of that. Be okay with taking time.

Finding the correct diagnosis for me was definitely a long process. Adam and I got married soon after my mission. Yes, he had full disclosure about what had happened and a chance to back out before I agreed to marry him. The first year we were married was a little bit rocky for me. I wasn't feeling great. I was still recovering from the end of my mission and had no energy to work or go to school. I felt like I was barely functioning. I finally went to see a doctor and he diagnosed me with clinical depression. I kept telling him "but I'm not depressed. I just have no energy and I can't sleep." The diagnosis did not fit in my head with what I thought was going on. I felt physical symptoms, I didn't feel sad. This was a good example of me having no understanding of what mental illness was. After lots of talking on his part and arguing on my part, he finally said, "Well, you're here because something is wrong." "Yes, I agree that something is wrong but I don't think I'm depressed." He finally convinced me that even if I wasn't, it couldn't hurt to try an anti-depressant because I was not doing well. I started on the medication. I hated being on the medication. I felt like I was lesser somehow than other people who could function fine without it. I also hated the side effects. It was frustrating for me to not be able to wake up in the morning. After taking the medication for a few months, I still felt like I was not seeing great improvement and the side effects were not worth it to me. I took myself off the medication (which you should never ever do on your own without a doctor's supervision) and didn't go back to see him.

I went some years dealing with the cycles of mental illness on my own. Sometimes I did ok and was able to handle it. Sometimes the symptoms were so bad I had a hard time getting through the days. The problem was that I wasn't stable. I would have brief periods of feeling fine (not superb but manageable). But I also had significant periods when I was definitely not fine. I knew I needed help. I started seeing a counselor to help work on some of my thought processes. I knew part of the issue was the perfectionist in me. I was so hard on myself, I put so much pressure on myself to accomplish things and be my best that I think the stress was eating away at me and that stress was causing intense physical symptoms. My body just couldn't handle all of that stress. After working through some of those issues with a counselor, I slowly started to learn to relax a little and to take it easy on myself. I learned to have more realistic expectations and be kinder to myself if those expectations weren't met. This did help some but I was still fighting with the symptoms and struggling through my days. I finally went back to the doctor and he started me on a different antidepressant. I seemed to be getting a little better for a while and I was hopeful that this medication would be able to lift the weight enough to be able to handle my life and be happy. This did not happen. The down cycles came back with a vengeance. I couldn't live like that anymore.

Growing up an athlete, I had always known the importance of taking good care of my body. I tried to eat right and we had good habits in our home. I don't ever remember having potato chips, sugared cereal or cookies in the cupboard. When I was younger, I thought sugar was of the devil. In fact I can hear my mom now eating her piece of fruit after dinner: "Mother nature makes the best dessert." Which I completely disagree with now. Chef John's Chocolate Molten Lava Cake made with Dove dark chocolate and fresh raspberries is the best dessert. My point being, I knew how important it was to take care of my body in order to feel my best.

I felt like I had tried the medication route (albeit reluctantly) and it did not work. I decided I would try a more natural approach. I started by visiting a reflexologist that a friend recommended who would work on my feet putting intense pressure on different areas of my foot that corresponded with the different zones in my body. The idea was to get the organs functioning properly and efficiently to help my body operate at its' optimum level. He told me that he would be able to help me with my problem. He assured me I would get better with his treatments. I went to visit him for months and tried to see some improvement. I did everything the reflexologist told me to do. I thought maybe I felt a little bit better, I wasn't really sure, but I kept trying and visiting him regularly. The down cycles still continued and I realized that this was not working. I needed more help than what this was providing.

I started using an herbal remedy and yam cream which was supposed to balance out my hormones. Don't laugh, all of this is 100% true. I rubbed the cream on the insides of my wrists twice daily and took the supplements faithfully for weeks. I didn't really notice much difference so I added aromatherapy to the mix and tried that for a while. I tried internal detoxes to get my organs functioning optimally. I still didn't see results so next I tried massage therapy (which I have to admit, I kind of liked. Getting massages weekly? Uh, yes please). I faithfully went and got worked on to try and clean out my body. Well months went by and other than my love for a good massage, I still didn't feel much better.

Next I tried acupuncture. I got treatments twice a week. The nice little Chinese lady promised me that she could fix my problem if I would just continue the treatments. I went for months and was still struggling. I felt like it was helping a little, but not enough to help me breathe. I needed more of the weight lifted. Just like the reflexologist, she was not able to deliver. I was feeling desperate so I found a homeopathic doctor who did an entire work up on me measuring all of my vitamin and hormone levels. This was a very comprehensive program and I was in his clinic for three days. At the end of the three days he showed me the results of all of my tests and assured me that this problem could be fixed. His exact words were, "There's nothing really wrong with you. Your only problem is that you had kids too close together." As if. But he did assure me he could help get my body back into balance. I went for weekly treatments in his clinic and took a lot of tinctures (which are liquid extracts made from herbs) which he also happened to sell. I bought them all and started the treatment with a renewed sense of hope. I also did talk therapy with him during some of my visits. More months went by and I was still having a hard, hard time. I was so discouraged that nothing was working but I knew there had to be a solution out there so I kept searching.

I found a naturopathic doctor who specialized in hormone balancing and thyroid treatments. He did another work up on me and told me I had an underactive thyroid and my hormone levels were off. He prescribed bio-identical hormones from a compounding pharmacy that made their own lozenges which were specific to my body and my needs. He promised me that soon I would be feeling so much better. More months went by and I did not get better. I was feeling more and more hopeless.

By then I was desperate. I was willing to try anything. I found a kinesiologist that did body memory testing. She worked out of a small office in the back of a health food store that sold all kinds of supplements and herbal remedies. My kids and I lovingly referred to her as Harriett the Witch Doctor. She too told me that this was an easy solution and I just had to follow her treatment plan. She found all sorts of areas that my body was deficient in and recommended more of the vitamins and serums which I was diligent about taking. They tasted awful but I was willing to do whatever it took to get feeling better. It did not work.

Keep in mind that none of these options were covered by insurance. I spent hundreds and hundreds of dollars and years and years searching for something, anything to lift this heavy weight. I gave every one of these options a solid chance and time commitment. I followed every directive I was told. Every single person told me they had the solution and in the end, none of them did. I was all out of options. There was not a single thing left that I knew of that I had not tried. I felt entirely hopeless. I didn't see any way my life would ever be better than what it was, which was not great.

I had a good friend whose husband was a pharmaceutical rep and he talked to me about one of the medications he represented that was used to treat bipolar disorder. He also referred me to a good doctor who specialized in mental illness. I was reluctant to try medication again. I had tried medication a few different times already and it hadn't worked. It had made my cycles worse. I didn't want to take medication. I didn't want to deal with the side effects. Even though I felt like that, I was at rock bottom. I had to do something. I figured things couldn't be any worse than what they already were. This was my last, last, last resort. I thought the worst thing that could happen would be a promise they could fix my problem and then have them not be able to deliver. Well, I had already been there for years so why not try?

I made an appointment to visit the doctor and this is what happened: I had been feeling really down when I set up an appointment with her for a few days later. When I went in to the appointment she asked how I was doing and I told her I was better. In fact, I had almost cancelled the appointment. She asked what I had done that day.

I told her "I went on a bike ride, did some laundry and washed my car."

She said, "Tell me about the bike ride."

"Well, I got up at 5:00 am and went on a thirty mile bike ride up Red Rock Canyon."

"Tell me about your laundry."

"Well, I washed and dried all the bedding in the house and I ironed all the sheets."

"Tell me about your car."

"Well, I detailed it so I took all my car seats apart and scrubbed the buckles, vents and hubcaps with a toothbrush."

She said, "Mequell, that is not normal. Normal people do not wash their cars with toothbrushes."

I told her, "People who like clean cars do."

"No Mequell, they don't. No one does."

It took a long time for her to convince me of this. From my perspective, this was just an example of me having a good day. This was my "normal" self. This was the level of energy and productivity that I measured all my days by and thought that I should be able to maintain that same level of productivity all the time. I actually never saw a problem with this high energy/high productivity stage. This is one of the reasons bipolar particularly is so difficult to diagnose. When I felt good, I didn't ask for help. I didn't think these high energy spurts were relevant to my diagnosis. Why would I? Everything was fine. The only time I asked for help was when I was so low I couldn't function. Every person I know diagnosed with bipolar was first diagnosed (and treated unsuccessfully I might add) with depression. Being treated for depression when you have bipolar does not work. Depression medication makes the bipolar cycles ten times worse. That is why I thought medication would not work for me. It turns out, I just had the wrong medication.

I wasn't sure how I felt about having a diagnosis of bipolar. On the one hand I had been searching forever for an answer to explain what was wrong. I had spent years being told that the problems were vitamin or hormone deficiencies or an underactive thyroid. I had spent years being told my body was just out of balance. I had followed so many treatment plans to correct this imbalance but still, I was barely eking a life out. I was miserable. I didn't want to have a mental illness. I would have preferred that the answer be one of those other things. However I knew that none of the treatments for any of those other things had worked. They had helped a little bit but not significantly enough that I had a better quality of life. I was not thriving. I was barely surviving. On the other hand, having somebody tell me they knew what was wrong did give me hope. Here was another avenue I hadn't tried yet. If this treatment helped me, then I decided I wasn't going to get hung up on whether or not I had a mental illness. I was desperately in need of help and if this helped, I was going to embrace it.

I started on the medication and within a few weeks, I felt significantly better. The intense lows of not being able to function day to day were not so severe. I was feeling more stable and was able take care of my kids and actually smile a little. I could breathe again. I definitely wasn't operating at 100%, maybe 60% but I felt like maybe, just maybe I could have a future—a future that would enable me to really live again. I didn't know how good I would be able to feel but I knew that I definitely felt better with this treatment than I had for years.

I wondered about how the doctor came to this diagnosis. I wondered if I had come to her years earlier, if she could have helped me and saved all those years of struggle because she would have known what to look for. She knew the right questions to ask. I wondered if I would have accepted a diagnosis of mental illness before I had tried every other possible route. I honestly don't know but I'm glad that by the time I got that diagnosis, I didn't feel like fighting it anymore. It wasn't like the first time around when my doctor thought I had depression and I didn't think he was right. I fought that diagnosis and the stigma of having a mental illness. I did not want to accept it. This time, my pride was all gone. I was looking for answers -- any answers that would help explain my symptoms and help me to take action and work to improve my life.

Before I had spent a lot of time searching for answers from anywhere but a psychiatrist. It actually never occurred to me to go see a psychiatrist. I thought psychiatrists were for crazy people and I knew I wasn't crazy. I never really considered the possibility of my problem being mental illness. Like I said earlier, I didn't know anyone with a diagnosis of mental illness. I didn't know anyone who went to a psychiatrist. I had a stigma in my head about what mental illness was and I knew I felt very real, very tangible symptoms. Being uneducated, I didn't realize mental illness is real and produces very physical, tangible symptoms. I didn't realize a psychiatrist might have the answers. As the years have gone on, I have been amazed to find out how common mental illness is and how many people I know who personally struggle with it yet no one wants to talk about it publicly. I know awareness now is much greater than it was before but with the general public, it still carries a stigma. No one wants to be open when they get that diagnosis.

Mental illness is difficult to diagnose mainly because it is impossible for a doctor to have all of the information that you have. We filter what we tell them things based on what we think is important, just like my experience when the doctor asked about my day. I had had manic episodes for years but had never given that information to a doctor when they asked about the problem because in my mind, it wasn't a problem. My brain working at warp speed helped me get a ton of things done. My energy level would go through the roof and I could go on very little sleep and get more done in a day than most people get done in a week. Honest truly. I thought it was fantastic. It wasn't until my doctor asked about areas other than the depression lows, when she asked about my energy and productivity (which I later came to find out was mania), that she was able to come to a correct diagnosis and see the entire picture. She knew the right questions to ask.

My husband Adam is a real estate attorney. One of the things he did regularly in the last recession was to consult with people about how to handle a deficiency on their home if they were under water with it financially. He has done hundreds of these consultations so he's very good at what he does. He knows what questions need to be answered even if the homeowner doesn't know the right questions to ask. There have been many occasions when he has finished with a consultation and the clients have told him that was the best money they ever spent. The reason why is because he answered all their questions. He answered the ones they asked as well as the ones they didn't because they didn't know enough to ask them. Specialized doctors are the same way. They know the right questions to ask even if we don't know what information is the most important to give them.

Mental illness is not something you can tackle on your own. You need a team. These are people who have your back and are just as interested and invested in your success as you are. A good doctor is the first person you need on your team. I think there are many wonderful, inspired, hard-working doctors out there. They specialize in different things. In my opinion, once you know you're dealing with some type of mental illness, it is essential to go see a psychiatrist. They have all the training of a family doctor plus a few additional specialized years of experience. They understand the intricacies of medication combinations and how to minimize the side effects. This is what they do and they're good at it. They know the right questions to ask.

It's important to find a doctor that you're comfortable with. Not all doctors are equal and you need to find the best possible one for you to be on your team. You need to be able to ask questions and know that they're invested enough to spend time helping you understand your situation. I've gone to doctors before that I felt just wanted the appointment to be over. They weren't interested in thoroughly understanding my situation or knowing anything about me personally. They didn't want to take the time to answer my questions. I was just a number to them and I knew they weren't invested in me. If you feel like that, that dynamic is not going to change. Go find someone else. It's ok to shop around for doctors. It's ok to give them a test ride if you will. Expect to pay for a consultation with each one but after the consultation, you can get a good feel for whether or not this doctor will be a good fit for you. I know it's hard to find good doctors. It's nearly impossible to find one if you're picking randomly off a list. Ask friends and family for referrals (I know, it's embarrassing but you can always say "I have a friend..."). It's helpful if you know other people who have struggled with mental illness. They can be your best referral source. Chances are, they've run the gamut and have experiences with a handful of professionals already that they can share their opinions on. Pick their brain and ask them what their best advice is for the stage you're at. You don't have to reinvent the wheel. You can glean information from them that will save you precious time in figuring out your next step so you can stop surviving and start thriving.

Once you've settled on the doctor you like, my advice is to bring someone close to you along for appointments. This is preferably someone who lives with you and can see first-hand how you are operating in your life. It is helpful for both the doctor and you to have another perspective on what is happening. My husband Adam is a great gauge and is very perceptive when it comes to my moods. Not that they aren't obvious. I don't always see it though. So when my doctor asks how I'm doing, I may not include everything that needs to be said. Also, when the doctor gives information for me about medication or things he wants me to try, it is helpful to have another brain on hand to recall some of the information later. Smart as I am, my brain is a sieve and I forget facts or instructions the doctor has given me.

This next tip is crucial and one most people don't ever think to do. If you do this, it will help you skip two spaces forward. You can advance to go if you will and collect your $200 without the pain of lumbering through the beginning stages of mental illness strictly by chance or the roll of the die. This will give you a head start and a reference point when you're trying to figure out your next step. Are you ready? Is the anticipation killing you? Here it is: Bring a notebook with you to all of your appointments and write down everything. This notebook should be your bible of sorts. This notebook is designated strictly for helping you learn and plan your next steps to improve your situation with mental illness. Bring it with you to all of your appointments with the doctor and later with a counselor. It's helpful to have everything in one place. When the doctor talks to you about your diagnosis, ask questions that you may have about it to help you understand that diagnosis better. Ask him what you can expect. When the doctor gives suggestions, write those down too. All of the key points from your meeting with the doctor should be written down in your notebook. That way you can refer to them after the appointment and remember the most important things that were said. I understand the doctor doesn't have an hour to meet with me so if he answers something that he doesn't have time to explain further, if his answer is a cliff note if you will, I put a star next to that topic in the margin which tells me I need to do some more research on that particular topic or question after I get home. It's amazing how much I think I can remember and then I leave and it's gone. All gone. If only I had written it down … There've been a few times I've had to call the office back or email the doctor for more specific instructions on something we discussed. Also, when you write it down, it forces you to ask more detailed questions so you understand it thoroughly.

This is another very important point. Ask questions--lots and lots of questions. Sometimes doctors start to speak " medical-eze" and I don't understand what they're saying. There are two issues at work here. The first issue is I need a doctor willing to explain. Look Mr. Doctor, it matters not to me how smart you are if you can't help me understand and improve my situation. That is what I'm paying you for. If you don't have time to answer my questions or are condescending to me in any way, you can't be on my team. The second issue is learning that it's ok to ask. This is information that is vital to your success in dealing with your problem. Don't worry about looking stupid. Chances are they've heard the question before and asking questions actually makes you look smarter. Very rarely are you ever the first person to ask a question that your doctor hasn't already heard. You'll either learn to communicate with your doctor better so you can get the most out of your visit or you'll find someone else and never go back so who cares what they think of you?

When I was out of high school and had just started college I thought that smart people just got it the first time around. Asking questions meant I was too dim to understand. It also meant that everyone else would see I was too dim to understand. I decided I would just work on it alone later. When I would leave class it took me ten times longer to grasp the concepts than if I would have just asked a clarifying question at the time. Now, I did well in school. I studied Sociology Research and Data Analysis with a minor in Statistics. I also had an academic scholarship so there *is* something going on upstairs. A few years ago I decided I wanted to pursue a graduate degree. I needed a few prerequisites so I took Physics and Chemistry. I am a lot older now than I used to be. Imagine that. So there was a big gap in age between me and the other students in class. This time around I was not worried about impressing anyone. I didn't care what the students thought of me and I didn't care what the professors thought of me. I just needed to understand the subjects. When I say I asked a lot of questions, that is an understatement. I raised my hand a lot and if I still wasn't clear I would speak with the professors privately during breaks or after class. I also went to the tutoring center. People may have been annoyed with me, who knows. But at the end of the semester, I got perfect scores on both my finals. Never happened to me before. I definitely understood the subjects.

This could be life and death that you're dealing with. At the very least it's the quality of your life. You need to understand. If you're unclear about what a diagnosis means, ask. If you disagree with the diagnosis, raise your concerns and tell him why. If he's using big words that you don't understand, ask what they mean. If you feel like the doctor didn't spend enough time asking questions to fully understand your situation, say so. If you've been given a prescription, ask about the side effects and the time frame before you should see improvement. Ask what you should do if you don't see any improvement by the end specified time period. If the medication helps you feel a little better but you're still not great, ask what the next step would be. Even though it's impossible to have an exact plan for everything, you should be able to see the next few steps ahead. Always have a plan.

After you are diagnosed, research, research, research. Ask your doctor for book referrals. Look for things on your own. Ask around and see if anyone else has experience with your diagnosis or knows someone who does. You'll be shocked at how many peoples' lives have been directly affected either through their own struggles or through friends or loved ones diagnosed with mental illness. Read everything you can to help you understand your diagnosis so that you know how to successfully live with your illness. I read all kinds of books about depression and bipolar disorder. Some were very scientific in nature and frankly, a little hard for me to read. But I still tried to get out what I could from those books. Some books were memoirs and talked about specific experiences with people and the onset of their illness. Some of these I could relate to, some not so much. Any time I could find anything though that rang true with me, I felt validated and understood. (As in see, I'm not the only one that feels these things.) What I never found though was a how-to guide. I wanted something that would walk me through, a step by step on how to succeed. That's why I am writing this book. I don't profess to know every answer for every situation but I do believe that there are some key principles that will help most anyone in dealing with mental illness. That is what I am trying to share. Some of the things I know to do now are not complicated or spectacular in any way but they are key things that make a difference in how I feel. I'm sure anyone that had lived with a mental illness for any length of time could have told me these things but they didn't. Instead, I felt like I had to reinvent the wheel. I had to try and fail and try and fail again before I understood that the keys to success are really very simple and it all starts with medication.

CHAPTER 3

MEDICATION IS YOUR FRIEND

• • •

GO AHEAD, SAY IT WITH me. Medication is my friend. I know in the beginning it's hard to believe that. No one wants to take medication. I get it. There are a lot of challenges and difficulties that come with taking medication. I am not unaware. We'll discuss some of these later but the fact is medication is the foundation of feeling better long term. In my experience it is impossible to improve on a consistent basis without it. Some may argue with me and feel that taking medication is a sign of weakness. Strong people don't need medication to function day to day. This is a fallacy. Strong people do everything they can to understand their situation and have the discipline to do whatever is necessary to feel better. There are many areas that will require your discipline and strength to improve your situation but fighting against medication is not one of them. Embrace it. I understand that taking medication long term is not without drawbacks. Ideally you wouldn't need to take medication but ideally you wouldn't have mental illness. Don't waste time wishing things were ideal. It is what it is.

Take whatever steps are necessary to do the best you can with the situation you're in. For me quality of life in the meantime trumped what may or may not happen long term with medication drawbacks. If you cannot live your life day to day and manage the simple tasks of taking care of yourself or your family, the weight is too heavy and you won't make it long term anyway. You need help lifting that weight. You can feel happy and live your life with purpose and meaning. Medication will help you do that.

Some people feel that medication is not only unnecessary but bad for you and a sign of weakness. They feel that natural remedies are the only way to go and that medication is introducing harmful chemicals into your body. They feel like medication just masks the symptoms instead of addressing the real problems. They feel like medication changes or masks the person's real personality. They just know that if you had faith and only used a natural approach to clean out your body and balance everything, your problem would be resolved. If this is you, come closer. Come in really, really close. Right there. Good. Now you're close enough so I can slap you! Look, you picked up the book and this is what I think. I absolutely will not budge on this one. The reason I am so adamant is because I used to think the same thing. I've told you about the difficulty of my finding the correct diagnosis. I've told you about all of the different avenues I tried to feel better that I thought would be healthier for my body. I've told you about my initial aversion to medication and some of the reasons I didn't want to take it. But I'm telling you now that this is the only thing that lifted the weight enough for me to become stable. Medication gave me enough help that I could breathe again. After I was stable and started to survive living with mental illness, I was able to take the next steps in managing my life so that I was truly able to thrive. You can thrive with mental illness but first you have to be stable. Proper medication is the way for you to become stable. Medication truly is your friend.

Even though I've told you this, you're probably going to go through the whole medication cycle. This is where you're at war with the idea of medication. Maybe you start taking medication because you're so low you're barely functioning as a human being. Your symptoms are so overwhelming you can't see past your nose. You go to the doctor and he prescribes a medication for you. You start to take it and maybe you see some improvement. You take it for a few months and feel like you're getting better. In fact, you're feeling better enough that you decide you don't need the medication anymore. You decide to go off of it since you're feeling better. Newsflash Einstein: you're feeling better because you're taking the medication. The medication is what's easing the burden. Do not go off of the medication because you think you don't need it anymore. When you go off the medication, you probably will feel ok for a little while. It takes some time for all the medication to work its way out of your system. You probably won't feel great but you get worse so gradually that you have a hard time being able to see it. It's like boiling a frog. Eventually you'll end right back where you started: barely functioning as a human being. Every time you go on and off a medication, you're making it that much harder for your body to become stable. When your symptoms return and you realize how poorly you're doing and decide to try medication again, it will take you that much longer to get back to where you were starting on your path to stability. Not to mention the six months it's taken you to go through the "I'm feeling better, off I go, wait no I'm not, give me back the meds" stage where you don't have a great quality of life. I also went through this cycle. I would feel better and start to feel stable. I still didn't want to be on medication so I thought the ultimate goal was to be stable enough to be able to get off the medication. When I started to feel stable, I would titrate off the medication. I would usually feel fine for a month or two after I was off. However the day of reckoning always came. I would go into a nosedive and crash more severely than before. Then I would realize that I definitely was not stable off of the medication. I would go back on to try and become stable again but each time I went through the cycle it took longer and longer for me to get back to feeling stable. Save yourself the time and stress on your body. You want to have a great quality of life. You want to thrive. Stay on the medication.

Another variation of the medication cycle looks like this: You feel terrible and realize you're not functioning well in your life. You know you need extra help. You go to a doctor and get a prescription then start on medication. You take the medication but don't see a vast improvement. What you do see are terrible side effects. I understand terrible side effects. I've felt so tired that I've walked into walls and couldn't hold my head up straight while sitting at a desk. It's no fun. I've felt that medicine-head feeling where it feels like my brain is working in slow motion and I'm trying to think but it's like seeing through mud. It stinks. I've put on twenty pounds in a month with absolutely no change to my eating or exercise habits. It's frustrating. I understand wanting to stop taking the medication because of these things. For all you business-minded people out there, this is like a cost-benefit analysis. Sometimes the benefit of what you get is far beneath the cost of what it takes to get that benefit. From the outside loved ones may see improved behavior or more stable moods. From the inside the cost of getting there dealing with the severe side effects are *so* not worth it. There is a way to manage the side effects. Feeling these side effects does not mean medication isn't worth it. Feeling these side effects simply means that maybe your dosage is too high. It means that maybe you're not on the best medication that will work for your body. All this means is you need more work communicating with your doctor to make some changes to find the medication and dosage that will work best for you. Remember, medication is your friend.

After you get your diagnosis, your next step is finding the right medication. When you are starting out, your doctor will suggest a medication based on what he thinks might work. He makes his recommendation based on what he knows about the medication, side effects and success with other patients. However, it is still just a guess. He doesn't know how your body specifically will react and how severe the side effects will be with you. He doesn't know if the improvement will be enough to make a difference. This is where you come in. Your observation and feedback will be the determining factors of whether or not to continue with that medication. Remember that you are all on the same team. He is not trying to force you to take a medication that does not work for you. It is not you versus the doctor or even you versus the medication. You are all working together to narrow it down.

This is the time to whip out your notebook and start to pick the doctor's brain. He will bring up a few medications that might work for you. Your job is to ask questions so you can decide together which medication you want to try first. The information you need to know is how this medication will affect you. Again, he doesn't know exactly but he does know the general side effects most people experience with any particular medication. Ask him what the side effects are for the medication he is recommending. You can decide which side effects you can live with and which ones you can't. Understand that there will be side effects that come with any medication so you're going to have to live with something. That's the bad news. The good news is that sometimes you can pick your poison (no pun intended). I've tried multiple medications and had different side effects with each one. Some of them I could live with (like headaches and tremors) some of them I couldn't (like weight gain and sleeping twelve hours). Again, ideally I wouldn't have to have any of these side effects from medication but ideally I wouldn't have mental illness. It is what it is. The stability to me is much more valuable than having an occasional headache.

When you and the doctor decide together which medication you're going to try, this is when you ask questions and take detailed notes. Ask what time of day you should take your medication. Ask whether it matters if you take it with or without food. Ask what side effects you should expect to see. Ask what you should do if these side effects become too severe. Ask how long it will be before you should see improvement. Ask what you should do if you don't see improvement within that time period. If you feel that the medication is not working or the side effects are too strong, ask how quickly and how much you should decrease the dosage. When you start on a medication for the first time, you generally titrate on. This means that you start with a small amount for the first week. The next week you increase that dosage. You keep increasing in small increments weekly until you get to the amount that the doctor feels will be the most beneficial for you. Take detailed notes about this. (This is the part where I would forget the instructions in the beginning of my diagnosis and I would have to call the doctor back. This is the reason I came up with the notebook bible.) Generally a doctor will prescribe a medication and then have a follow-up appointment with you for 3-4 weeks later after you've titrated all the way on. I've also had some doctors request that I email them a week or two after starting the medication before my follow-up appointment just to see how it's going in the beginning. When you leave, you should have a very good idea of what to expect with your medication.

Understand that medication takes time to work. I know it's not what you want to hear but it's the truth. It's like exercising.

When you start to work out you might feel a little bit better but it's not like your cholesterol immediately drops forty points. It takes consistent, daily effort of making better food choices and exercising your body for the change to happen. Medication is not an overnight life changer. Doctors will tell you that when you start a new medication you should expect to see improvement in one to two weeks. This is when the improvement starts but for me it took much longer to reach the highest level of improvement the medication was capable of. I understand it's hard to take medication day after day when the only immediate results are overnight side effects that make life miserable. When you don't see immediate improvement it's hard to convince yourself to hang in there. Let me just say that it is worth it. Finding medication that enables you to live your life feeling good is worth the time and effort it takes to get there. The key is consistency.

You need to follow the doctor's instructions exactly. You need to be committed to consistently taking your medication. If you take it for a few days then forget a few times, you're not going to get an accurate representation of whether or not that medication is a good match for you. You need to take your medication at the same time every day. In the beginning, I had a hard time remembering because I wasn't in the habit of taking pills. I bought myself a pillbox to put next to my bed so I would see it first thing when I woke up in the morning and last thing when I went to bed at night. This is generally when the doctors will recommend you take your medication. Having my pills right next to my bed along with a water bottle made it easy for me to remember to take them and be consistent. Alright, I have to admit that I absolutely hated having that ugly pillbox next to my bed. It didn't go with my décor. My bedroom is painted and decorated to look and feel like a relaxing spa. It's very zen-like. Laugh if you want but this is a true story. You may not care about your pillbox matching the décor in your bedroom but for me every time I looked at that ugly pillbox it made me clench my fists and grit my teeth. Definitely not conducive to my relaxing spa feel. For me, this story had a happy ending. My son Max knew how I felt about that pillbox so he searched far and wide and found me a cool, sleek, black pillbox that looked like a notebook on some urban hipster website. Now whenever I look at the new pillbox it puts me back in my happy place. Very zen-like.

Once you have your medication system in place, the real work begins. This is when you get to start charting (see index). Tracking through charting is imperative! This is the best way for you to monitor whether or not the medication is working. Charting involves at the very least recording when you take the medication, how much you take and how you feel that day. It can involve much more as time goes on. When my doctor first brought up the idea of charting I felt so overwhelmed I couldn't even think of it. It was about a year before he could convince me to try. He printed out a mood chart that looked very complex and gave me stress just having it in my hand. However it turned out to be not nearly as bad as I thought. You can find mood charts online. Pick whatever layout you're most comfortable with. Just make sure it has the basic information of which medication you take, how you felt that day and a line to write daily notes so you can keep track of the side effects. The chart that I used was very comprehensive and in the beginning was way too much for me to do so I simplified. I scratched out the preprinted medication names and wrote the name and amount of my medications. I simply checked the box when I took them and before bed, I would color in the box that measured my mood that day. I kept the chart on my nightstand next to my bed with a pen along with my pillbox so it was easy to remember and do. Keep those systems in place. Set yourself up for success.

My charts go back five years. In the beginning they were very elementary. As I got more comfortable with the charts I started adding more elements. My next addition was to write the time I took the pills instead of just a check mark. I also added what time I woke up and how many hours of sleep I got. These columns were not all in the chart so I scratched out some of the headings and wrote in the things I wanted to track just so I was using the same chart and it would be easy to find what I was looking for. I also wrote notes in the top section that helped me monitor the side effects and see if there were any other circumstances that may have affected my mood that day. For instance, if I was crazy busy or had company at the house, I may have been in a bad mood but that was not because of medication which was important to know when monitoring side effects and moods.

Tracking through charting was the single most impor-tant thing that helped me in determining what was and wasn't working with medication. It also helped me get a more accurate picture of what was really going on because sometimes I was so down it felt like nothing was working. I felt hopeless. I really did forget what it felt like to feel good. Having my chart showed me literally that last week I did feel good and it was in ink to prove it. It also helped me identify trends and other areas that affected how I felt. Now I track a lot of things. I track whether or not I exercised and if so, what kind. I track how irritable I felt with the kids. I track whether or not I took a nap and how long it was. I track whether or not I had a headache that day since dehydration is one of the side effects of my medication. I track when I am on my girly cycle which helped me identify an important trend. The week before my cycle is generally more volatile than I would like. I used to panic over this and think my medication wasn't working but after tracking, I recognized the trend. Now when I start seeing moods ranging outside the norm, I check where I am during my monthly cycle and if it's the week before, I relax for a few days and don't worry about it. I'll watch the cycles and see if I still feel off the following week but 99% of the time, it's just a few days of more extreme cycles. It fixes itself when my girly cycle is over. All of this helps me identify how to feel my best. Don't worry about starting this all at once though. Begin with the medication, moods and side effects. Tracking that will help you identify whether or not the medication is working.

So now you've got your medication. When you are starting that medication and charting the side effects to see how severe they are along with charting your mood you will be in a position to more accurately measure what's working. If you see that you slept fourteen hours after taking 450 mg then you know the side effects are too severe and the dosage may be too high. You have proof in black and white both for yourself and for the doctor. If you see that your moods are not changing much, the dosage may not be high enough to make a difference. Again, what you need is evidence. This is kind of like my daughter coming to me when she was younger and complaining that her brother was mean. If that was all she had to tell me, nothing much was going to happen to him. But if she came to me and said he was mean because he stole her blankie and ripped the head off of her bear and she had the decapitated toy with stuffing falling out that proved it, he was going to be in a lot of trouble. Same thing with doctors. Doctors will take you a lot more seriously when you have backup to show how you feel and what is going on. It will also show him you are serious about your condition and willing to put in time and effort to improve the situation. He will take more time to talk with you if this is true. Without a chart it's hard to remember specifics and if you tell your doctor you hate the medicine and don't want to take it but can't tell him why, he doesn't know where to go with that. You need to be able to tell him specifically why you don't like it, exactly how it makes you feel and how much and when you're taking it. When you give him this information he has enough information to make an informed decision about changing.

Along with bringing your notebook to every appointment, you should also bring your charts in to show your doctor. Once

I started seeing a psychiatrist, he would request that I send over the latest chart before my appointment so he had time to review it. This helped him to be prepared and know ahead of time the areas we needed to address. Remember that doctors only care as much as you do. If you are flippant about your condition or flaky about showing up to appointments or inconsistent about taking your medication, doctors will not spend as much time trying to help you. They can only help so much. They can advise but they cannot make you take medication or make you take good care of yourself in other areas of your life. If you are dropping the ball in these areas, the doctor cannot help you. Don't be the weak link in your team. You make sure you're doing everything in your power to become stable and control the areas that you can control. Your goal is to thrive.

So the next question when starting a medication is deciding when to pull the plug. At what point do you decide this medication is not working for you and you need to try a different one? There are two reasons that you would make this decision. The first reason would be you don't see enough of a difference in your mood. The weight is not being lifted enough. This decision should be made together with your doctor. Ideally you should give the medication four to six weeks before making this decision. You should have had follow-up appointments with him or email communication along the way and tried adjusting dosage amounts to see if that would make it work. You want to make sure you've tried everything to make that medication work before deciding to pull the plug. It's not bad to pull the plug, you just want to make sure you are 100%

certain that this is not the best medication for you before doing it. Don't feel like it's wasted time or you are back to where you started. You actually have valuable information now because you know that whatever medication you tried is not the best fit. You have eliminated something from your list. Some medications work in similar ways. Medications that work with the same receptors in the brain are grouped into what doctors call "families." When you eliminate one medication you can generally eliminate all the ones that are in that medication family so by eliminating one, you are eliminating a whole group. This puts you way ahead. Picking your next medication to try will be more educated and less by chance. Again, make sure you are working with your doctor. You need the doctor to help you because you will have to titrate off the medication. This means decreasing the medication a little each week until you are entirely off. It generally takes two to three weeks to do this.

The second reason you would decide to pull the plug would be because of side effects. If the side effects are not something you can live with, make a change. If you have a severe reaction to the medication, you should pull the plug immediately. This is the only time you should ever stop a medication cold turkey. This should still be done while working with the doctor. One time I had a severe reaction to my medication. I had moved across town so I was looking for a doctor closer to my new home. I found one but she was concerned about something in my medical history interacting with my medication so she wanted me to make a change. I was feeling stable so I was very hesitant about doing so but she was insistent. I asked her all the questions about this new medication discussing side effects and dosage amounts. After being on the medication a week or so I started getting a rash on my stomach. I didn't think much about it because sometimes I get allergies and rashes were not on the list of side effects we had discussed. Well the rash kept spreading and after a few more days it had spread all over my torso and up my chest and to my face. It dawned on me that this could be a side effect from the medicine. I hadn't done my own research on this new medicine, I had just written down the side effects that the doctor had told me. After looking on the pharmaceutical website for that medication, rashes were one of the first side effects listed. I called the doctor immediately but could not get a hold of her so I left a voicemail. She still had not called me back by the end of the day so I called her emergency number. When she finally called me back the next day (after blisters had shown up on my face by the way), she told me that it was not possible for me to have this reaction to the medication and she was upset that I called her emergency number. She had never had any other patient react that way and have this particular side effect. Well, I didn't really care about any of her other patients and how they reacted to this medication. I only cared how I reacted and it was not good. She was fired from my team. Not all doctors are created equal. I called my previous doctor back and decided it was worth it to me to drive across town and have someone on my team who listened to me and would respond when I needed help. He advised me to stop taking the medication immediately.

Changing medication is a slow process. Do not take it lightly. For me it generally took a few months to make a complete change from one medication to the next. I have had doctors do it slightly differently but for the most part it looks like this: two to four weeks to slowly titrate off the current medication since stopping cold turkey is a baaaaad idea and you should never do it, one to two weeks to get the old medication completely out of your system, two to four weeks to titrate on to the new medication and feel the full effects. In the meantime, you can expect to sleep for a large part of your day because weaning off a medication tends to do that. When I was making medication changes, I looked ahead at my calendar and (if possible) waited until I had a good solid two months clear from holidays, company, final exams or summer (since my kids were home and having their friends drop by while I was asleep on the couch at noon in my bathrobe with my greasy hair was embarrassing). If you don't have to worry about this then yay for you. Take advantage of that and get to work finding the best medication for you.

I've had friends that have tried medication but didn't feel like it worked for them. They were still at war with themselves and wondered if medication was something they wanted to take anyway. They tried one medication and made their decision that medication was not the solution based on that one experience. Understand that it generally takes a few tries to find the right medication for your body. Don't make your decision without exploring all of the alternatives. Also understand that if you don't have the correct diagnosis finding the right medication will be much more difficult. If you've tried a few medications already and haven't found anything that worked, it might be worth talking to your doctor about your diagnosis. There may be other symptoms that you haven't taken into consideration or told your doctor about that will help lead your doctor to the correct diagnosis. Don't throw in the towel yet. Keep plugging away and eventually you will find a medication that will help you significantly in lifting that weight.

Changing medication is also a little unnerving. Back when I was still sorting through medications trying to find the best fit, I was making a change and I had a hard time trying to decide whether or not I liked the new medication and whether or not I thought it was working. I had started on one originally but was still seeing a lot of swings in my mood and energy levels. I wasn't stable enough. The doctor and I decided we would try a new medication so I started the process of titrating off the first then onto the second. When I started on the new medication I felt different. When I was on the original medication, I felt a little drugged all the time. I felt numb and a little bit brain dead. My energy levels were still very volatile. I didn't feel like myself. Starting on the new medication was very different. My energy levels were much more consistent which was good but my brain felt wide open. I don't know how else to describe it other than there was a lot of room in my head. It was much harder to keep a proper perspective and not panic. I didn't like it at first but I stuck with it and once I got used to the open space in my head, I liked it more. I felt stronger that I was able to control my thoughts. Remember that different isn't necessarily bad. Give yourself some time to adjust before making decisions on whether or not to stay on a medication.

Another thing I didn't realize was that one medication is generally not enough. When you're dealing with mental illness, most of the time you end up needing a medication cocktail. This means that you will be taking a combination of different medications. The first medication that you will take will be your anchor medication. Once you find the right fit for your anchor medication, something that helps significantly in lifting your weight, you can start to add other medications to help you feel even better. Right now I am taking an antipsychotic, an antidepressant and another one to counteract the side effects from the first two. I'm not even lying about that. Obviously when you have more medication variables it's harder to track which one is having what effect. This is why you only add one medication at a time and chart. You need to be very sure that it's a good fit before moving to the next step. When I first was diagnosed, I was only on one. It helped significantly but I still didn't feel great a lot of the time. It wasn't until I added the second that I felt stable and once I added the third I felt great. I still have some side effects but because I track with so much detail, it is easy to go into my doctor and show him my charts and have him make educated suggestions that work. For instance, once I went in and told him I was angry a lot of the time and I also couldn't wake up in the morning. He increased one med by 10 mg which is a very small amount and changed what time I took my pm pill by a few hours so that the sleeping effects would wear off earlier the next day. That is the kind of fine tuning a good doctor can do but he can only do that if he has very specific information about what's going on with medication, moods and so forth.

I know I figuratively slapped some of you for being anti-medication and pro-holistic healing. I want you to know I don't think medication and holistic healing have to be mutually exclusive. It's true that I don't think a holistic approach can lift enough of the weight on its own. I tried it for years and came to that conclusion. Based on my own experience I think medication is required to lift the bulk of the heavy burden of mental illness. I do however think that a holistic approach *in addition* to the medication can help significantly. I believe in taking care of your body. I believe in vitamins and supplements. I think that balancing your body and cleaning it from the inside out are extremely helpful *in addition* to the medication. Just make sure that you are committed to the medication first.

Committing to medication is a very personal issue. You are the only one that can make this decision for yourself. You may have doctors or loved ones that are pushing you to go on medication. This is because they love you and they truly want to help. They believe this is the best thing for you. Understand though that they cannot force you to make this decision. You yourself have to believe that this is the best route for you and you are committing to it. This is your choice. Doctors and loved ones cannot micromanage you into taking medication against your wishes. They can try but if you don't personally want to do it, you will fight back either passively or openly.

This will become a huge issue between everyone. You will not be consistent with taking your medication. If they are not right next to you handing you the pills and watching you swallow them, you won't take it. This will not help you. If you are not consistent about taking the medication, you will not have an accurate representation of whether or not it's working. If you are not 100% committed to this and want it for yourself, don't bother starting the medication route because it won't do you any good. Take charge of this decision in becoming stable with your mental illness. Use your brain. Don't doubt your intellect. You are still capable of making this decision.

As a side note to loved ones here, you need to recognize that you are not in charge. I know you're probably very frustrated watching your loved one struggle with this heavy burden. However you need to have a clear understanding of your role. You are there to encourage and support. You are there to be a cheerleader. You are not there to fix their problem and no amount of pushing on your part will get them to do something they don't want to do. They are still capable of deciding for themselves what steps they want to take to try to address the heavy weight. You can weigh in on the issue and share your opinion on what you think will help but you can't make them have the same opinion. It is helpful for you to help them do homework on doctors and medication if that's what they want. Ask them what kind of help from you they would like then listen to their words and respect their wishes. Doing this will take the power struggle dynamic out of the picture. This will put you back on the same team. Once your loved one knows you are there to help in whatever capacity they want your help in, they can focus all of their energy on improving their situation instead of spending it fighting against you.

So back to you. You are in charge. Be smart and educated about what you choose to do to help you improve. Make the choice for yourself. P.S. if you want my two cents, I vote for the medication.

CHAPTER 4

SUICIDE

(And How to Avoid It)

• • •

BEFORE I EVEN START HERE I just have to say don't be all judgy. If you think you can read this with an open mind be my guest. I'm happy to help you see this from an insider's point of view. But if you're already judging because I call myself 'an insider' then put the book down and back away slowly. I mean it. You may think I'm irreverent in my light hearted comments about a serious subject, but believe me, I know the gravity of this topic. I figure there are two ways to handle it. I can either laugh or cry. I've done my share of my crying and frankly, it gives me a headache.

I'm a two-fer. That means two attempts for those of you who are a little slow in the head. (Do I need to include that neither was successful?) Suicide is not exactly what you think. I never wanted to die I just wanted everything to stop and didn't know how to accomplish that. I had tried everything I could think of to feel good again and nothing worked. This was simply the last thing I knew to try that was on my list. I have to say if it had worked then I would have been successful in getting everything to stop. Granted I would probably be seeing clearly then and would have panicked over what I'd done and been trying desperately to undo it.

Making the decision to take your own life when you're struggling with mental illness seems like a very logical decision from the inside. It's not just because someone is "crazy." It's been well-thought out with people weighing the pros and cons of their situation. It's probably taken a long time for them trying to manage this heavy burden on their own before that decision is made. It's also a last resort. No one jumps immediately to this conclusion. They try everything they can think of to feel better first. It's just that nothing seems to help enough to make a difference. There's a panic that happens when they realize they have no control over how they're feeling. They have no way of making a difference in this crazy new reality that they're in. There's nothing they can do to control it. There's nothing that will help it to ever get better. They think this is what their future looks like for the rest of their lives. It's a very bleak and hopeless picture.

I remember talking to Adam very calmly telling him what was going on in my head. Taking my life made perfect sense to me. It was actually the most logical thing I could think of in solving this problem. I felt I was so preoccupied with trying to survive myself that I didn't feel like I was a very good mom. My kids were young and needed a lot of time and emotional support. I didn't feel like I was in a position to offer either.

I was grumpy and impatient whenever they needed anything and since they were kids, they often did.

I felt like I was a huge weight for my husband, that I was making him deal with all my issues and inadequacies. If he had a different wife, someone who didn't struggle with mental illness he would be so much better off. I want to say that he never made me feel like that. He was a wonderful, supportive and loving person. He was very encouraging and kind whenever I was struggling and tried to help me see all the good that I did. He told me what a good mom I was to our kids and what a good wife I was to him. I just didn't believe him when he said that. I looked at what I thought was the evidence. I wasn't taking care of basic things around the house. I didn't have the energy to do the dishes, do the laundry, clean up after anyone or help when they needed things. The kids were on their own a lot of the time to handle meals, homework and other issues in their lives. They were still very young and I thought that it was too much to ask of them to lift this heavy burden that I was placing on them by my own inadequacies when it wasn't even their fault in the first place. I was the one who couldn't handle everything. I was the one with the issues. I was barely functioning myself. I was barely surviving. I was sleeping for hours and could hardly wake up in the morning. I would stumble out of bed and attempt to oversee the kids getting out the door for school. It was a pitiful effort really. I would just lie on the couch in my bathrobe and tell them what they should do next. After they got out the door I would fall back asleep on the couch for a few more hours. It wasn't much of a life. And I honestly didn't see it changing any time soon.

I had been stuck in this downward cycle for so long that I never thought I would feel better again. I had been struggling desperately for months. Nothing was helping and I didn't see that changing. I didn't know anything else to try that could possibly help me. I knew I was barely making it through the days trying to take care of myself and my family. My goal during that time was to just make it through one more day. Be alive at the end of the day. Just don't die that day. That may not sound like much to people who don't suffer with mental illness but for me this was a monumental task. This goal was so big, not taking my life for one more day, that each hour was a battle. I was exhausted. I knew I couldn't live thirty or forty more years with this kind of weight. This burden was too heavy. I knew my days were numbered. I felt like I was eighty years old. I was so weighed down with physical and mental exhaustion, guilt for my inadequacies and despair that nothing would ever change that I was completely hopeless. There was no way for my situation to improve. I had tried everything. I had done it all and it wasn't enough. There was nothing left to help me. I was out of options. There were no other logical choices left.

I didn't feel like I was giving up when I was thinking of taking my own life. I felt like I was being proactive. I felt like I was making a conscious choice that would improve my own situation and the situations of everyone around me. I felt like I was taking control and solving a difficult problem. I knew I didn't want to live in my current circumstances for thirty or forty more years. I didn't want that future. Given the choice between living with that future or ending my life, I felt like ending my life was the more reasonable, more logical choice. I knew that the people around me would probably be sad at first, but eventually they would get over it. They would be so much better off that I was doing them this favor. I thought that they too would be glad I'd made this choice once they moved on with their life and had a better wife and a better mom to take care of them. I thought they would be relieved that they wouldn't have to deal with the burden of mental illness anymore that they didn't choose and they weren't responsible for.

When I hear of people committing suicide, I've often heard their loved ones say that it seemed like they were getting better. They had been doing poorly before but for the last few weeks, they really seemed to be on the upswing. I think this is because they finally felt like there was something they could do to change their situation. They had plans to make a change. They had taken back some control over what was going to happen for them in their future. Control is the thing that people struggling with mental illness feel like they don't have. They don't have control over the cycles. They don't have control over their moods and their energy levels. Making the decision to take their own life gives them back some control.

I spent a long time pondering over my situation. Deep down, I didn't really think I could outlast the bipolar. I figured I could buy some more time but that was all I could really do. I knew how it would end, it was just a matter of when.

So I spent a lot of time thinking about a smooth transition. When I was doing laundry I would tell Adam "If you get married again, make sure she doesn't put your jeans or t-shirts in the dryer or they'll shrink." "If you get married again, make sure she knows that Sam needs lots of encouragement when he's doing his homework." "If you get married again, make sure she has the kids clean their own bathrooms." I gave him a lot of instructions on what his new wife should do. I just knew that everyone would be so much better off with someone else filling my role.

After I had spent some months reflecting on this issue, the end finally came. It started off innocently enough. I had a friend invite Adam and I to be part of their Ragnar Relay team for a race coming up in March. We both like to stay in shape and this sounded like fun to me. Adam had previously run a marathon and I had just finished another triathlon a few months earlier. We figured training would be a breeze. This turned out to be a very poor decision... For those of you who don't know what the Ragnar Relay is, I'll fill you in. It is a roughly two hundred mile race run by a twelve member relay team. Each member of the team runs three separate legs so it breaks down to about five to seven miles per leg making each runner run between fifteen to twenty miles. This in and of itself is a feat but added on to this is the relay portion. The race starts sometime Friday morning and you run continuously through the night until the race is finished the next day.

We had our team separated in two different vans by legs. The first six legs were in van number one. I was the first leg out. Our race started in Wickenburg, Arizona where I ran the roughly six miles. After the start of the race the van drove to the next transition point where runner number two (Adam) got out to wait for me. After the handoff, we took off to the next transition area where we waited with leg number three and so on.

At each transition area the team would get out and cheer the other runners on. It took us most of the day to get through the first round of legs. My second leg was in the evening and after finishing I felt medium. My knee was bothering me and I was ready for bed. But wait, there was no bed. There was only a big white van filled to capacity with six sweaty, stinky bodies. Up ahead you'll read my words about the importance of a bedtime. Well this race is the reason for my rule. We cheered our teammates on until the wee hours of the morning when we finally stopped at a high school gym to catch a few hours of sleep while the second van with its runners was making the rounds. (And when I say a few hours, I really do mean a few ... as in two or three). I was shaken awake around 5:00 am to frantic whisperings of my teammates as our second van was ahead of schedule. We all grabbed our sleeping bags and jumped in the van then jammed on to the next transition to start it all again.

As the second day ran its course, we were all very excited to be done and all twelve of us ran across the finish line together. I left the race with a participant medal, a matching t-shirt and complete annihilation of all my physical and mental resources. I was kaput. If I had had a week to recover I think I could have pulled out of it but as it was, there was no rest for the weary. I came home to three little kids who needed a mom and house that needed one too. The next day was Sunday which was always a hard day between my primary[5] calling and a husband that was gone all day for his responsibilities.

The week started with everyone back to their crazy schedules. I remember we had something on the calendar every night of the week. I told Adam that I needed a break. It takes a while before I get to the breaking point but once I do, that's it. That second. I'm done. Adam said if we could just make it through Saturday, we could schedule some time off. There was a missionary lesson he needed to attend and there would be a baptism on Saturday that he had been working with the missionaries on for a number of months. I understood this was a big deal and I didn't want to be the weak link.

I managed to get through the next few days but it wasn't pretty. I think I actually heard the 'crack' in my head. It was too much. Saturday after the baptism (yes I showed up and smiled like everything was fine) I couldn't take anymore. I could feel everything in me giving out. I took a bottle of pills and locked myself in the bathroom. I could hear the chaos of everyday life going on outside the door and I knew I didn't have it in me. I swallowed every single pill then slumped down onto the floor. It was such a relief to know that this would be over and I would get a break. As I laid there I felt like I was traveling down a long tunnel. The noises around me kept getting farther and farther away. I heard Adam come in the room

5   Children's class at church

and he dropped down next to me. He tried to get me in the car to go to the emergency room but I refused to go. I could hear the panic in his voice. He called an ambulance and we made quite the spectacle with fire trucks and police cars all wailing their sirens on to our tiny street.

The strongest emotion I felt was a huge sense of relief. I knew that today something would change. Throughout the rush to the hospital and once inside the emergency room I was nonresponsive but I could hear everything going on around me. I could hear the worried whispers of the doctors and nurses. I could hear the beeping of the machines. I stopped breathing. I could feel consciousness slipping away when suddenly I had a thought. If I fell asleep I knew I was going to die. It startled me, the finality of that thought and I suddenly realized I had a choice. This wasn't the only solution to my problem. I had people I loved and a life worth living. I didn't want to die, I wanted to live. It was as if a fog lifted from my brain and I was able to see clearly. I started to fight to stay awake and it was difficult. I had periods where I stopped breathing but the doctors managed to keep me present.

After a few hours I started to stabilize. Adam came in the room along with our bishop.[6] Our sweet bishop who is also a doctor kindly asked "Mequell, what happened?" It was difficult to speak because I was so drained but I managed to get out "I don't know. I was sitting there minding my own business when the pills jumped into my mouth." Not even a smile. I thought to myself are you kidding? Do you have any idea how

---

6 The local leader of our church congregation.

much energy it took to make that joke? That's when I knew I would be ok. I would be ok both in the short term and in the long term because I knew, I KNEW I didn't want to die and I would never make a choice like that again.

This experience has given me valuable insight in how I live my life. I know now that when I recognize I need a break, that means now. I can't make it another week. I cancel as much as I can immediately. Sometimes it's difficult because I don't feel like I can cancel. What about visiting teaching[7]? Or preparing a lesson[8]? Surely those things can't be cancelled. Actually friend, they can. Or just reschedule them, or ask someone to sub for you. Do you want to know what happens if you don't do them? Nothing. The world does not end. This is true for most anything in life I can think of. My favorite question to ask myself when I feel backed into a corner with a demanding, hectic schedule is this: "What is the worst possible thing that will happen to me if I don't do (fill in the blank)?" Sometimes the absolute worst thing that will happen is I might look bad to other people. That's something I can live with. I don't want to be thought of poorly but given the choice between that and being stable, I pick stable. People may understand or they may not understand but either way, I'm ok with it.

That was something I really had to let go of and I think it's a good thing. Other people's opinions of me do not matter. If I

---

7 Women in the church are assigned to visit other women each month to check in and see how they're doing.

8 Members of the church are sometimes asked to teach lessons from manuals at Sunday meetings.

am right with Heavenly Father, then that's it. He understands my burdens. He knows the intent of my heart. He sees the effort I put in each day. At the end of my life no one will be asking my neighbors what they think of me. Only one opinion matters.

As I've reflected over this experience, I came to learn some very important things that will (hopefully) keep me far away from the cliff's edge. One thing I learned is it's impossible to make a good decision when I'm tired. This is true both physically and mentally. I remember when Adam and I first were married. The cute sealer[9] in the temple told us to never go to bed angry with one another but to instead, talk it out and clear the air. I think that could possibly be the worst piece of advice I've ever been given. That may work for other people but personally the only thing that happens when I try to solve anything late at night is the problems get even bigger and hairier. If I go to bed and address it in the morning, sometimes the problems have resolved themselves and I get to save all that wasted brain power that would have gone to trying to find a solution. Call it avoidance tactics if you will but it really does amaze me how many times I have a big fat problem that I can't seem to figure out that magically shrinks to a manageable size after getting a good night's sleep. Sometimes in the morning the problems seem so small, it takes seconds to figure out my next step. That to me seems like working smarter, not harder.

When Max was a freshman in high school, he was on the wrestling team. He was also taking three Honors classes which

---

9 One authorized to perform marriages in a Mormon Temple.

produced a lot of homework. One night his teacher's quorum[10] went to do a service project for a homeless shelter and he didn't get home until late. This was after his typical day that started at 5:00 am for "A" hour at school. He had wrestling practice directly after school that lasted until 6:30 pm (normally) but he had to leave early for his service project. By the time he got home at 9:30 pm he was exhausted. He sat up at the table where his math and chemistry homework were spread out. I was finishing the dishes and I looked over at him to see how it was going. He was sitting with the chair pushed back from the table, arms dangling down by his sides, legs sprawled straight out in front of him and his head leaning back against the top of the chair with his mouth wide open. That was the exact same position he had been in five minutes earlier when I'd checked. So I asked "How's it going?" He responded with a long, despondent sigh that sounded something like a balloon deflating. "That good? I feel ya." He said he still had to finish a packet for geometry, a packet for chemistry, study for the chemistry final, finish the reading and notes, make his lunch AND he was one and a half pounds over-weight and there was a wrestling match the next day. There seemed to be no solution to finishing this amount of work. My advice? Go to bed. Get up and address it in the morning. If you stay up to try and finish this, it will take ten times longer because you're tired. Your mind is not firing on all pistons because it's out of gas. If you go to bed and get a good night's sleep, in the morning

10   Church group of 14-15 year old boys

your mind will be fresh and you can whip through your list of things to do in no time. I had pity on the poor kid and helped him with his lunch and he decided to work a short time then go to bed. In the morning when I drove him to school I asked how he was doing. He said (with a huge smile on his face) everything was much better. See? Sleep is magic.

It's amazing how many situations can be fixed by sleep. My kids are fighting? Go to bed. You'll feel better after a nap. Homework is too hard? Lie down for a few minutes and address it when you're rested. My kids tease me because I think the solution to any problem is sleep and I go to bed pretty early. Bedtime is my favorite time of the day. Really though, it's like a magic pill that's guaranteed to cut your worry and stress in half (at least). And it's free. The next time you have a problem that you just can't seem to solve, try it. Go to bed and see how small your problem seems in the morning.

When you're struggling with mental illness and you're at the scary point of contemplating taking your own life, realize that you are in an exhausted mental state and shouldn't be making any big decisions. The thing you need is a reprieve from the depression which is why suicide actually seems like a good idea. Nothing else has worked. I want to tell you that you can get a break. This feeling is not forever and it will end. You just have to hang in there a little bit longer.

A great example of this was at my son's wrestling match over at the high school. I noticed that the wrestlers did this for their teammates. When some of the teammates were on their backs very close to getting pinned and the time was almost out during a two-minute period, the other wrestlers on the side would yell "Short time! Short time!", meaning fight it out, don't give up, you only have seconds to last. If you can make it, you get a fresh start at the beginning of the next period. What encouraging words! I feel like telling that to people when they're struggling and can't seem to shake it. "Short time! Short time!" Just keep putting one foot in front of the other and remember to breathe. That's all you have to do when things look bleak. Don't worry about your to-do list. Don't worry about the mountain of things that are pushing you down. Put your head down, take a deep breath and make it through the day. If you can do that, celebrate and congratulate yourself on making it, then go to bed. Don't think about how long this might last. Don't worry about how you're going to solve the problem. Just make it through the day. You can do anything for one day.

I really learned this lesson a few years ago when I decided to up the ante and do a long course triathlon. This race was going to be in Show Low, Arizona up at Fool's Hollow Lake in the mountains. The swim portion was 1.2 miles. Now I had done many short course races before. I had also done a handful of open water swims both in the ocean and in smaller lakes. I spent hours training in the pool and knew I could easily finish that distance. At the start of the race I donned my wetsuit since in the early springtime up in a mountain lake it is FR-EEZING. Now swimming in a wetsuit made me a little claustrophobic. It was tight around my neck and made me feel like I couldn't breathe. So I'd taken it to the pool with me for a few training sessions to get more used to it. But I almost died of heat stroke since the pool was a toasty 85 degrees. But that's beside the point. I was treading water at the beginning of the race with a few hundred other racers. The bullhorn sounded and I stuck my head in the water and started swimming. The first quarter of the race was spent dodging kicks to my face since we were all still swimming in a pack so I didn't have much time for my mind to wander to anything else.

After we settled into our rhythm and spread out a bit I expected to quickly get in the groove and stride it out. But it didn't happen. I kept swimming but the wetsuit was tight around my neck and the water was pitch black. I started freaking out. I thought about how long I had already been swimming and I wasn't even close to being done. I thought "O.M.Gosh. I am half a mile out in the middle of a lake and I think I might die. They will never recover my body." Now I've had a few panic moments during open water swims but if I just flip on my back for a few minutes, I can talk myself off the ledge and get back in the race. I don't know what my deal was this time but it was not working. So instead I concentrated on my breath. Stroke stroke breathe. Stroke stroke breathe. (Yes, I breathed every other stroke because at that point I was not worried about my time, I just wanted to make it out alive.)

I'm happy to say I lived through the swim. I felt great on the bike but by the time I got to the run I was back to my panicked thinking that this was something I didn't know if I could do. I had been racing for hours and I still had miles to go. I remember thinking that those miles still sounded like forever. So

I broke it down again in my head. I stopped thinking about the miles left and started picking out landmarks ahead. I thought I'll just run up to that rock up there. After I would get to the rock I would look ahead and pick out the next landmark. I'll just run up to that sign. After I made it to the sign I thought I'll just run up to that turn in the road. I was able to finish the entire race that way. Breaking it down in my mind enabled me to successfully complete the race.

It got me thinking though about looking too far ahead. Before the race I thought that when I was swimming, I could just think about the swim and not worry about the bike and run. That would be broken down enough in my mind so I wouldn't get overwhelmed about how long the race was going to be. I didn't realize that I would have to break it down to much, much smaller increments for my mind to stay focused. Stroke stroke breathe. That's how small my increment had to be in order to make it through. That is why I say make it through the day. Don't worry about the years or months or even weeks. Make it through one day. Don't even worry about tomorrow, just make it through today. I promise that you will get better and soon it won't be so hard. How does that happen? Read on.

CHAPTER 5

THE ENERGY BUDGET

• • •

Don't laugh. It's a thing. Alright maybe I'm the only person I've ever heard of refer to it this way but that doesn't make it any less of a thing. Learning how to manage my energy budget was absolutely crucial in figuring out how to not only survive but thrive with mental illness. This is the secret sauce if you will. If your energy is so depleted and you are in that dark, suicidal place, what you need is a break. You need to figure out how to get more energy in your budget. Recognize that this crisis is temporary. It will not last long. You just need to figure out how to get through this short time period until you can catch your breath again.

The first thing I recommend is cancelling everything that you can. When I say that, I am not suggesting you simply drop the ball and don't show up. I am suggesting you call someone to make other arrangements for whatever it is that needs to get done. You don't want to leave other people in a lurch or have assignments not addressed. That will put the people around you in a bad spot and if it happens frequently, they will be less likely to help when you need it. When I say cancel everything, that really does mean everything like carpools, making dinner and other household chores, outside events, even church callings.[11]

A few years ago I was having a rough go of it. I felt overwhelmed, stressed out and on the brink of despair wondering how much longer I could do it. I had two callings at church. I taught Relief Society[12] and was Gospel Doctrine[13] Class President. (I opened up class and called on people to say prayers. I am not even making that up. It's a real fake calling). They were not big ones but they did require me to be there and be in front of people every week. I couldn't see any way out of everything that was on my plate. The kids were all busy in sports and I had carpools to keep up with, running the house with cleaning and meals, work, church callings, etc. After realizing I was at the breaking point and knew I needed to take immediate action, I decided to get a sub for my next lesson in Relief Society. I stayed home "sick" that day. I even got someone to open up class for me for the next few weeks. Well, I knew I couldn't be there if I'd asked for subs so I planned a fake trip just to get out of going to church. Now I normally don't miss church. I'm pretty much there every week. It was about this time that my husband stepped in with his wisdom. He said "If you're making up trips and missing church just to get out of doing your callings, something needs to change. Maybe you

---

11 Members are asked by church leaders to serve in different positions in the church. This is referred to as a calling.

12 Women's class at church

13 Sunday School

should ask to be released." After I threw holy water on him and told him to "Get thee hence Satan" I thought about it. Maybe there was truth in what he was saying. When I was feeling well, I loved these callings and I didn't want to give them up. However, I did know that he was right about changing something. I decided to call the Relief Society President and let her know my limitations. I told her about dealing with bipolar and that I was going through a difficult time. I told her how much I loved teaching Relief Society but I was not able to do it for the next little while. I wasn't sure how long that would be. It might be two weeks or it might be two months (it ended up being two months by the way). If there was any way to have subs cover until I was back up on my feet that would be great but if that wouldn't work out and she felt it was best to release me, I understood. That conversation went a long way for me feeling like I had an ally on my side who understood my situation. She said no problem, she'd get the subs and to let her know when I was feeling better. It also helped me not feel so alone in dealing with my illness.

In trying to get a break, I am also a huge fan of pajama days. These are days when I really have cancelled everything on my schedule and I get to do nothing. Sometimes I put on clean underwear and then put my pajamas back on but sometimes I don't. (You've already agreed not to be judgy so remember that before forming an opinion). Then I do nothing. Or something. Whatever I feel like. Sometimes I read a book on the couch all day. Sometimes I putter around cleaning things up. Sometimes I go to yoga or go out to lunch with a friend (they have to be a really good friend because remember, I'm still in my pajamas). If you work, consider taking a sick day but remember, use it wisely. If you are in dire circumstances and really need a break, take the day to lie on the couch and watch three movies in a row. Whatever would give you the most relaxation, that's what you should do. If you have small kids at home, cash in a favor and ask a friend to take them for the day. You can repay them by bringing over a store bought chocolate bar which is the least stressful way I know of to say thank you without adding "make homemade cookies" to my list which would negate my afternoon off.

This is actually a fun part of planning your break. You get to imagine the thing that would be most relaxing to you and do it. There's excitement in anticipating a break and doing something that helps you. This is where people's breaks look different. What's relaxing for me may not be relaxing for you.

I have a friend who is very social. She likes to plan big events and is always on the go. She'll spearhead kids days at the park and organize bringing in deli sandwiches and split up the cost for thirty people involved. She plans kayaking trips and bike rides. In fact, her nickname is "The Cruise Director" because she's always got something fun in the works. When she and her husband go on vacation, she likes to get up early and go go go - to museums, historical sites, etc. Her husband likes to relax and read a book. After years of tug of war on vacations, they came up with the Travel Constitution. This states that they can each do whatever they want on vacation without any guilt or pressure from the other party. My point here being, what is relaxing for her is not relaxing for him. Figure out what is relaxing to you and put that on your list. Maybe it's sitting in your room listening to calming music on your headphones. Maybe it's taking a drive up the canyon all by yourself. Maybe it's spending the night at a hotel or even your mom's spare bedroom where no one will ask you to do anything and no one can get a hold of you. Remember that this is only for a short time. Your goal here is to get through the immediate crisis. Do whatever you have to do to get your feet back under you.

Once you're out of the danger zone, you need to step back and take serious stock of your life. What put you into the danger zone in the first place? What does your schedule look like? What kinds of demands and stressors do you have in your life? How much help do you have in the things that need to get done? You will need to start shuffling around and adjusting things to make sure you do not get back into the crisis zone. This means you are going to have to do some things differently. You're going to have to learn how to manage your energy budget.

Before my second suicide attempt, I was on medication. I had learned previously that it was fundamental in helping me to survive. I thought taking medication would allow me to live my life exactly the way I had before, always busy, always pushing. What I hadn't learned yet was that I would need to do much more work in addition to the medication in order to stay away from the edge. I hadn't learned how to manage my energy. That suicide attempt for me was a big wake-up call that I needed to make some huge changes if I wanted to thrive.

An energy budget works just like a financial budget. The same key principles and elements apply. You have to prioritize where you want to spend your energy, monitor your budget as time goes along, make adjustments along the way and most importantly, do NOT overspend. It is vital that you stay within your energy budget. If you keep pushing even when you feel like you're at the end of your energy that is what leads to the dark, scary place. That's what puts you in a crisis. If you can figure out how to stay within your energy budget you can live a long, happy life even with mental illness.

The most important thing to recognize is that energy is a finite resource. There is no such thing as unlimited energy. Thinking that you have unlimited energy and pushing yourself to constantly do more or be more will blow your energy budget. You need to acknowledge that there is a budget and that when you go over there are dire consequences. Other people may be able to be more lax with this but when you have mental illness it is essential for you to stay within your energy budget. If you go over it could be a life or death situation. Going over your financial budget regularly is a bad thing. It could lead to bankruptcy or other serious financial consequences. However going over your energy budget regularly could be worse. It could lead to suicide. Do not overspend your energy.

When you have mental illness you have to be more acutely aware of your energy budget. Don't look around at other people and compare your energy budget with theirs. That's great if someone can take dinner in to other families in the ward, host large social gatherings at their house, and serve on every committee that sends a sign-up sheet through Relief Society or at school. You need to realize that this has nothing to do with you. Don't worry about comparing yourself to them. They are in different circumstances than you are. They are managing their own energy budget and if that's a price they can afford to pay then good for them. Comparing yourself to other people is a useless endeavor that causes a lot of unnecessary stress.

After I graduated from college, I worked at an ad agency in the research department. We did a lot of market research trying to find out which ads were most effective. One thing that is fundamental to understand in statistics is that you can't compare numbers or draw conclusions unless the surrounding circumstances are identical. If you are going to compare market research with surveys for example, the questions have to be asked in exactly the same way. Asking "What color do you prefer, red or blue?" is not the same question as aking "What is your favorite color? Fill in the blank." They look similar from the outset but because one is open-ended and one limits the answer to one of two choices, this question cannot be used to draw similar conclusions.

You may look around at other people and think that your situations are similar. You may think that you should be able to do all that they're doing. That comparison is completely irrelevant. You can't compare yourself to anyone else. Your circumstances are not identical. Your energy budget is your own. All you can do is do the best you can with what you've got. Sometimes it's tempting even financially to look around and think "Heeeey wait a sec! They go to Hawaii twice a year.

We should be able to go to Hawaii twice a year too!" You can't look around at other people and compare your spending. Everyone has different financial budgets. Energy budgets are different too. Understand how much energy you have to allocate to different areas in your life. The size of your budget isn't the key to happiness. How you spend the energy in your budget determines whether you're happy or not.

If you are spending your energy on things that are the most important to you in your life, you will feel a deep sense of satisfaction and happiness. Spending your energy on your top priorities is what brings you happiness. It's not necessarily bad to have a smaller energy budget as long as you spend your energy wisely. You will need to prioritize the very most important places that you want to spend your energy and stick to that. That will bring you fulfillment and joy. Remember the size of your budget does not determine happiness. Too often we spend time wishing and lamenting that our budget isn't larger instead of spending our time figuring out the smartest ways to stay within our budget. It would behoove you to spend most of your time figuring out how to stay within your particular energy budget instead of fighting and complaining over the fact that you wish your energy budget was larger.

Another key factor in staying away from the edge is recognizing what puts you there in the first place. I am a homebody at heart and I like to have time to putter around my house. I feel good when my house is clean, the laundry is done and I have food in the fridge. It helps me relax and handle a busy schedule when I can come home to a calm, peaceful environment. For this reason, we don't have TV or video games. I know that sounds extreme but for my family it's a way of keeping chaos out of the house. If my schedule gets so busy that I can't take care of my responsibilities at home, that's no bueno for me. I also know I can't have something scheduled every night of the week. If I'm out of the house two nights in a row, it throws me in a tailspin. I say no to a lot of things in order to keep my evenings calm.

Be ok with saying "No." This is a huge challenge in our "can-do" world and service oriented church. There are so many activities and projects that are good, worthy causes but if I said yes to all of them, I would be dead. As the years have gone on, my list of things that I say yes to has been whittled down. I say yes to callings and to visiting teaching. Sometimes I have to modify the calling or let them know I may have limitations and if they still want me, great. I say no to watching kids or bringing in home cooked meals (although once in a blue moon, if it can't be helped, I'll buy a Costco chicken and bagged salad). That drains all of my emotional energy and there are other ways to serve.

When I get up in the morning, I like to think of someone who could use a friend. Sometimes I'll call them on the phone. Sometimes I'll show up at the door with a chocolate bar (Lindt dark chocolate with oranges and slivered almonds in case you're wondering). Sometimes I'll write a note. The point is there are ways I can serve that don't drain me. I don't have to say yes to every opportunity that comes along to be developing Christlike attributes. If you find you are drained constantly, figure out what the biggest culprits are and either eliminate them or change them in a way that will work for you. You can get a break.

Another issue to address is the shoulds and shouldn'ts. What I mean by that is don't spend a lot of time or energy worrying about how things should be or how things shouldn't be. For example it shouldn't be hard for me to get out of bed in the morning. I agree. In a perfect world it shouldn't be. But I have to deal with facts and reality. The fact is it is hard for me to get out of bed in the morning because I am so tired from the medication. Acknowledge that fact, figure out how you're going to manage the situation better and move on. Don't feel guilty. Don't compare. Don't worry about it. It's wasted time and energy and you need to use all the energy you have in smart ways. Feeling guilty, comparing, worrying about how things should or shouldn't be are not smart ways to use your energy so stop! Forget about it! Or if you're from New Jersey "Forgedaboudit." Recite this in your head so you can repeat it to yourself when you get stuck in your own mind. For example: It shouldn't be hard for me to serve in a time consuming church calling. Well it is. Forgedaboudit. Now what are you going to do to alleviate some of that pressure? I should be able to keep my house clean and cook three meals a day. Well you can't. Forgedaboutit. Now what are you going to do to manage that? (May I suggest cold cereal for dinner at least twice a week? If you feel bad throw in a multi-vitamin.) Once you've dislodged all those wasted emotions that come with the shoulds and shouldn'ts you can use that energy to address the problems. In saying this, I'm not suggesting you ignore those limitations and push through. I am saying acknowledge and respect the limitations and figure out what you're going to do to address it but don't worry about them or spend time wishing they weren't there. That is a useless exercise that like I said, wastes your energy.

If you have someone telling you what you should and shouldn't be feeling or doing, they need to wise up and understand how heavy and difficult this weight is. Have them read this and have a frank discussion with them about how this is affecting you. In order to do this, you need to firmly believe that your struggles are not because you are a bad person or because you are inadequate as a human being. These are medical issues that can be addressed. You tell them they are adding to your stress, adding to your guilt and not offering any kind of solution. Just because something is not hard for them does not mean it isn't hard for you. This is like you treading water in the middle of a lake with 40 lbs. sandbags around your neck while someone else jumps in the lake unencumbered and swims laps around you all the while telling you how lame you are for struggling to keep your head above water. Sure they can do laps, but they don't have sandbags. We're not talking about the same things and if they can't understand and appreciate what you're dealing with I'm happy to accidentally-on-purpose throw a carton of eggs at them until they can see the light. I am passionate about this point! If they're not helping then they need to think before they speak. Don't judge or criticize something that they obviously don't understand.

The only words that should be coming out of their mouths are words of encouragement.

There was a time period before I was stable on medication when I was expecting my second son that I was seriously struggling. I had a two year old and I was in the depths of depression and in the middle of a very rough pregnancy. I didn't have the energy to do anything. I would drag myself out of bed in the morning and go downstairs where I would get breakfast for Max then fall on the couch because I was so sleepy and could barely function. He would watch PBS all day (if I tell you it was PBS I feel better about myself than if it was the Cartoon Network being educational and all, you understand). I would lie there and sleep until it was lunchtime when I would drag myself off the couch to get some more food for him. After I would fall back on to the couch and sleep until my husband got home from work. I felt terrible. I felt terrible both physically and mentally. I didn't understand why I couldn't wake up or why I had no energy or why I couldn't function. I knew this was not normal and I felt like I should be able to do these things. There was no reason I should be lying on the couch all day. I felt like I was a failure. I felt like a complete waste of skin. I thought I was a terrible wife and mother. I felt like I was lazy and if I would just discipline myself I should be able to have energy to do things. I knew I should exercise and clean my house and study my scriptures but I was not physically capable of doing any of these things. The longer I laid there, the worse I felt.

When Adam would come home from work and I was still on the couch sleeping in my pajamas, I would feel awful. I would apologize for being such a terrible wife and mother. Instead of criticizing me or worse, confirming any of those feelings, he would give me a big hug and say "Don't worry about it. Your job is to grow a baby. That's it. That's all you have to do and you're doing a great job!" He made me feel like I was still a worthwhile human being and loved and valued.

You are still a worthwhile, valuable person who can contribute to your family and your community with your insights and wisdom. Don't discount what you have to offer. Don't feel bad thinking that what you have to offer is not enough. There are people you can help and ways that you can serve that are unique to you. No one else can help in the same ways you can help. I love when people come to me after being diagnosed with mental illness looking for some guidance and direction. This is something that I can help with because I've gone through the same thing. I love the feeling of being able to share things that I've learned. I can help people specifically because of mental illness where other people can't. This makes it feel more like a blessing than a burden because I can help people that I otherwise would not have been able to help. I understand. I get it.

Recognize that your best is good enough. That lesson, that my best is good enough even though I fall short, is one of the most important ones I've learned in my life. I know that's what the Atonement teaches but actually internalizing that lesson and truly believing it is difficult. I know that I don't have to be perfect, I don't have to excel, that I can in fact be very mediocre and the Lord will still be pleased with me if I am putting forth my best effort. That's a hard lesson to internalize because inevitably we look around at other people to gauge where we are. What level should I be at? Am I keeping up? Am I on track and progressing the way I should? Sister Whats-Her-Bucket[14] serves as Relief Society President and takes meals to people twice a week and keeps her house cleaned all the time and has her kids looking cute with ribbons in their hair and matching jewelry (not the boys, that would be weird). She takes cookies to new ward members and invites neighbors to listen to the missionary lessons and keeps up a blog where she bears testimony and shares wonderful stories about her kids who never fight. There are a million things to look around at and compare other people's strengths to our weaknesses. Stoooooopppp! Don't do it! There's no point in comparing yourself to anyone else.

Our whole goal in life is to become the very best versions of ourselves. It doesn't matter what someone else's best self looks like because they are not you. You are not required to do the same things as they are to become the best version of yourself. Heavenly Father will direct you on the things he wants you specifically to do. Don't get caught up in the rest of it. It doesn't matter. I heard a wonderful quote that IF I cross stitched, I would put on a pillow. "Only do the things that only you can do." Don't stress about the rest. Delegate.

---

14 People in the church refer to each other as "Sister" or "Brother." For example, I am called Sister Buck.

That's what kids are for. Realize what you can realistically do and what you can't, then make adjustments accordingly. If you're wondering what it is that only you can do, ask Heavenly Father. He will tell you every day what it is he wants you to do even if it's something very small like phoning a friend in need.

Thinking back to my mission president though, I know the only reason he was able to take away the rules and all the pressures that went along with them was because he knew 100% I wouldn't abuse that. He knew I would still study my scriptures. He knew I would still bear testimony and find and teach investigators. He knew I would still pray with my companion and work hard. He knew he could count on me to be obedient to gospel principles. He knew me. All he did when he removed the rules was take away the pressure and help me to feel that what I could do was enough.

Last year I had a similar situation with my daughter Ella when she was eleven. I am very big on teaching my kids independence and personal responsibility. They do very well managing their lives. Now Ella is a real go-getter. She's bright and happy and energetic and loves to be involved. When school started that fall she decided she wanted to be involved in (what I thought was) a ridiculous amount of things. She was on student council and the Principal's Advisory Committee. She was on the Yearbook committee and was a member of the National Honor Society. She signed up for Battle of the Books which required a ton of outside reading. She also played soccer on the All-Star team at nights and on the weekends. She lined up and fulfilled all twenty of her required service hours for National Honor Society within the first two months of school.

All of these things required regular outside-of-school meetings and extra time commitments. She got herself up early and to all of her meetings on time. She set up her own meetings with the teachers when she needed to make work up or needed extra help. She let me know what days she would be staying after school and when to expect her home. She gathered all of her own gear and got herself over to where her carpool left from when it was time for soccer. She truly did manage her own life. While doing all of this, she also maintained high grades and was on the Principal's Honor Roll. Crazy, right? Well about three months into school the pressure was getting to her. The meltdowns were starting to become regular. So I talked to her. I asked her what she was most worried about and she unloaded. She talked for half an hour. She was so stressed she was going to get a B and that would make her ineligible for the coveted Principal's Award at the end of the year. I said "Ella what is the worst thing that will happen if you get a B?" She was quiet and just looked at me. I said "Nothing Ella. Nothing will happen if you get a B. It will be ok. You don't have to get the Principal's Award to be a good person." The visible change in her countenance was immediate. She looked at me with her big, sad blue eyes with tears streaming town them and just stared. "I mean it Ella. It's ok to get a B."

I could say this to her because I knew her. I knew that she would push herself and strive to do her very best. She would study hard in school and finish all her homework and prepare for tests. She just needed to have the pressure removed. She hugged me and smiled. We talked about the most important thing in life which is personal growth. She was growing and reaching and striving already. She was doing a great job. Incidentally, she still ended up with straight A's and got the Principal's Award.

Your best really is good enough. You don't have to do it all. Don't worry that you can't do everything. You can still say yes to things that are important to you. You just have to figure out a way to do it and still stay within your budget. The key is understanding how "expensive" things are to you in terms of energy and working in a way that will allow you to spend your energy where you want without blowing your energy budget. When we first moved into our house and I was decorating (which I happen to love by the way), I found a beautiful picture of Michelangelo's painting of The Creation. I was so excited to bring it home and put it up on my wall. I just knew it would be perfect. When I got it home and hung it up, I realized that the proportions were all off. The painting was not nearly big enough to balance out the size of the wall. I took the picture into a framing shop to have it matted and put into a larger frame. The quote I got on that was $800.00. Yeah right. I got the painting at a discount store for $150.00. No way was I spending that. But I still needed to figure out a way to have the picture take up more wall. So I went to my favorite store (Home Depot) and wandered around the aisles. I found some beautiful crown molding that I thought I could work with and a few cans of spray paint. I came home and busted out my saws and made that crown molding into a larger frame. I treated it with a few different painting techniques until I got the look

I wanted and then painted a large square on the wall to look like matting. When I hung the picture back up inside my new frame and faux matting, it was perfect. It was just the look I was going for and it only cost me $40.00. I got exactly what I wanted and I didn't blow my budget.

Managing your energy works in exactly the same way. When I was called to teach Relief Society I was a little nervous. The teachers that had taught before me always had beautiful displays with things they brought from home, homemade hand-decorated sugar cookies and elaborate handouts that went with their lesson. I knew that if I did lessons like that I would blow my energy budget. That was not something I could keep up with. I said yes to the calling and figured out a way to do it that worked for me. I spent 100% of my time focusing on the lessons and the right questions to ask so we could have a good discussion. My priority was teaching a lesson where people felt the Spirit and came away with personal revelation for them to work on in their own lives. I taught for three years. I never once made a handout. I never once brought treats. I never once brought visual aids or decorated the table but I still felt like I was able to bring valuable insights to the sisters in that calling. I contributed in my own unique way and most importantly, I didn't blow my budget.

When you have mental illness you need to be very protective of your budget. Your goal is to have energy to spend in ways that make you feel happy and that help you serve other people. Spending your energy makes life enjoyable just like spending money is enjoyable. The key factor to both is making sure you spend the right amount. You need to get in the sweet spot. Don't overspend your budget. Don't push it to your absolute limit. It's nice to have a little cushion of both energy and money because sometimes there are unexpected issues. If you spend every last penny during the month when something unexpected comes up like repairing the dishwasher or the car, you're in trouble. It's ok to spend the majority but you don't need to spend every last penny you have financially. The same thing is true with your energy. Don't spent every last bit of energy that you have. It's not required for you to do that. It's okay to have a little energy left over to use in case of unexpected things coming up. Spend your energy doing things purposefully. Decide what your priorities are and spend your energy there.

The whole idea is to have the time and energy to spend on the things you want and on the people who are most important to you. If you already love what you're doing and feel invigorated by your choices then you probably don't need to read this book because you're doing just fine. But if, I suspect, you feel the demands are too great and you're exhausted trying to meet all of them, maybe you're spending your time in the wrong places. This doesn't mean that you can't do anything, it just means that you get to choose the things that are most important and that give you the most energy and satisfaction when you do them.

Let me give you an example. I love spending time with my kids. Let me tell you, they're a blast. We have so much fun together. We go kayaking, rock climbing, hiking, cliff jumping (to the chagrin of my very conservative, danger-aware husband), camping (with or without said husband) and all sorts of things. My favorite thing to do during the summer or on a school break is wake up and say, "What can we do today?" and think up an adventure. My car is the perfect size. It seats seven which means there's enough room for me, my three kids and a friend for each one. Last winter break we decided to hike Picacho Peak. We woke up early in the morning, drove around and picked up all our friends then headed toward Tucson. If you're ever in the area, this is the most fun hike I've ever done. Hands down. Period. You climb up to the saddle then down the back side using cables. Then you get to rock climb up to the summit using cables. Seriously the bomb. We spent the day racing up the mountain, lunching at the summit and playing around.

That afternoon as I was dropping friends off, one of the moms came over to chat with me and she said "I don't know how you have the energy to do things like this." I was a little taken back because she is one of the most amazing women I know and seems to have unlimited energy with all things domestic. I could never keep up with her homemaking skills and projects. I thought about it and realized two things. First, this for me gave me energy back. It was fun and I got to be active, outdoors and spend time with my kids. Second, I am very specific about where I use my energy. I know that I can burn out quickly and don't take on things that will do that to me. The key is knowing how much you have in your budget and deciding where to spend it. You can ask yourself questions like "If this was my last hour of energy to spend for the day, what do I want to do with it?" Occasionally I'll cook a nice meal but once the meal is done, I'm out. Dishes get (mostly) done by the kids or Adam and the rest will wait until the morning. Sometimes my kids want me to jump on the trampoline with them and we'll have sandwiches or cold cereal for dinner. Very rarely do I spend the last hour of my energy on something that's not a high priority in my life.

Every so often there are times when I'm up against a deadline with something that needs to be done now with work or meetings outside my home and I just have to cowboy up and get'er done. These have to be the very rare exceptions or I will burn out. Just like with my financial budget, I get irritated when I feel I've been monetarily committed to something that I didn't want. I also get irritated when I get backed into corners with my time. I don't want other people committing me to things that are not the highest priority on my list. That's not how I want to spend my energy. It makes me salty. This is why I learned to say no and I'm not afraid to say it. I don't want anyone else choosing how I spend my energy. I want to save it for my highest priorities that allow me to live a long, happy life where I get the breaks necessary to keep on going.

I've had to get creative in figuring out the smartest ways to use my energy and where it's ok for me to cut. There are some things I've cut out that before I thought were mandatory like putting on make-up and doing my hair. I don't know why doing those things makes me feel stressed out but I hate spending forty-five minutes every morning doing them. I feel like it's wasted energy and when I'm low, those things don't make the short list. Usually I'll shower and get dressed but I have no problem going out and about in sweats and no make-up with my hair in a ponytail. I realize that some people won't be ok with that. I gave up worrying about what other people think long ago so I just do what works for me. I figure as long as I look nice on Sunday and date night all the other days primping is optional.

It really is ok to say no to things. There is never a shortage of good causes to donate your money and energy to. At Adam's office last month one of his coworkers had organized a food drive. Another one was raising money for a cancer walk. We had just had a ward fundraiser for the young women trying to earn money for girls camp. Financially we all understand that we can't donate to every good cause that comes along. People typically don't go into debt in order to donate to charity. People understand and know their financial budget. If they've already donated to a cause that month they don't feel bad about passing up donating on another cause. They look at their bank account and if they don't have the money, they don't worry about it. If they had more they'd love to donate but at that point they just don't. People don't respond the same way with spending their energy. They feel much guiltier about saying no because there's no financial price tag to it. They think they should be able to do it all. You don't need to do it all. You don't need to say yes to every worthy cause. Before saying yes to something assess how you feel and what your energy levels are, then determine if you can do it or not.

If someone needs a meal or there's a signup to help clean someone's house ask yourself if you're in a position to do that.

If the answer is no, don't worry about it. You need to count the cost. If the cost is more then what you have take a pass and let somebody else do it. Maybe you'll have more energy next time. You don't have to do everything that's good. That's an impossible feat and will burn you out. Don't worry if other people say yes to everything. It's no good comparing. Just do what you are capable of doing.

Try to look at your energy budget more analytically like you would your financial budget. Remove the emotions and the guilt and do accounting periodically to assess how you're doing. Charting will help with that. If your chart is not stable or you have not been doing well for the past few days then you are low on energy and it is not a great time to overextend and do big projects. If you take a step back and build your energy back up you will get to a point where you're feeling better. At that point you can step in and take a meal to someone or help with a service project. Before you commit, count the cost and determine if you have the energy for that commitment. If not don't feel guilty, just pass on it until next time. There's nothing wrong with that. Everybody has limitations in different areas. There's nothing wrong with having a limited budget. At some point everybody has to say no to something. Even people with large budgets have to say no to things in order to stay within their energy budget.

If you are saying no to commitments to stay within your budget then that feels empowering and noble. Without this perspective saying no makes you feel weak and inadequate. Staying within your energy budget is being proactive. It's a positive thing. When other people ask for things that you are not able to do say it doesn't fit within your budget right now. Controlling your resources is important and is a priority. It's a good thing. Saying no isn't always a bad thing. Help people understand and don't feel bad about it. Treat it methodically. Take the emotion out of it. If you focus on doing what the Lord wants you to do then that is a top priority where you can spend your energy wisely. Heavenly Father doesn't blame or become disappointed when we say no to things because we're staying within our budget. First and foremost he wants us to be good stewards over ourselves. Be self-sufficient and be in control of your lives. Know what your energy resources are and spend less than you have. That's what pleases him more than taking on too much and burning out. Realize that you're pleasing God by staying within your budget. He understands different people have different budgets.

I'm reminded of the story about the widow's mite. The amount that she had to give the Lord was very small in comparison with other peoples' donations. She had a tiny financial budget but the Savior put her on a pedestal as an example. To me that story shows that it's not about the quantity or size of our budget that pleases the Lord, it's what we do with it. How do we spend the limited resources that we have? Mental illness usually means you have a smaller energy budget. The important question is how do you spend that energy? Do you spend all day on the computer on social media or socializing or serving outside of the family? First and foremost you need to take care of yourself and your family. You may have to trim out what others can fit in. Figure out what your top priorities are and spend time on those. Sometimes instead of cleaning the house, I focus on relationships with Adam and the kids by spending time with them. Sometimes I can do both but not always. I have the energy that I have. It's how I spend it and what my priorities are that defines the happiness and satisfaction in my life.

There may have to be some major adjustments in your life for you to effectively manage your energy budget. It's also important to realize that your energy budget is not entirely individual. It's a joint budget with the rest of your family. When your family is committed to things that means you are too whether it's through carpools or taking on the extra load at home if your spouse is gone or just the mental effort that comes from being responsible for one more thing. When I am feeling overburdened and close to the edge, Adam also cuts back. He delegates what he can and spends quiet time at home. This helps me to not burn out. Our family has made major adjustments in order to stay within the energy budget and that's ok. Don't feel bad that the people around you have to change things in order for you to stay healthy. I truly believe it's been a great blessing and learning opportunity for my husband and kids to see outside themselves and understand things they can do to help our family succeed.

This is another area where we've had to get creative in figuring out how to do things to stay within the budget. As you already know, I love sports. I love watching my kids participate in them and work hard at achieving their goals. But being signed up for multiple sports makes our family life crazy. We decided that we would only sign up for one sport per season with the kids rotating whose turn it is to participate. Our family can only handle one sport at a time. When they were younger, we also signed up for sports that had practices in our neighborhood so the kids could walk and get themselves to their own practices. Max has taken guitar lessons for the past seven years and our solution for that was to find a teacher that could come to our house for the lessons. This way I am not committed to driving every week in addition to the sports Ella and Sam are participating in. There is a way for everyone in our family to have their needs met without burning me out. We just have to think outside the box.

I am very good at managing my energy now but I still have periods where I my energy varies. However if I am aware of that I can use the swings to my advantage like planning for some of my big, dreaded tasks and saving them for when I'm manic. I have a large list of big projects I'd like to do around the house. It sits by the phone where I can refer to it easily. But the key here is I don't look at it daily. This list is saved for days when I am looking for a project and want to dig my hands into something big like steam cleaning my garage floor and defrosting and cleaning the garage fridge and freezer (which by the way, I tackled last Saturday because I was manic). I have a separate to-do list that I make for each day with things that ideally will get done. I make this list the night before. The next morning when I wake up, I gauge how I feel. Do I have a lot of energy today? Or is it a pajama day? If I have a lot of energy I get started on my list. If I don't, I start crossing things off. This can wait until tomorrow. This can wait until next week. Sometimes I'm left with only one thing on my list that absolutely has to get done that day. Sometimes there is nothing left on the list and I can relax. Realize that managing your energy is dynamic in that it's constantly changing. Be in charge. Learn how to manage your own energy budget. Do not overspend. Learn how to restore and get more energy. These things will allow you to live your life on purpose so you can thrive.

CHAPTER 6

THE BASICS: EAT, SLEEP AND EXERCISE

• • •

THERE ARE MANY THINGS YOU can do to recharge your energy over time. I learned this the hard way which is why I'm so determined to share this with you, so you don't have to. I didn't understand the simple things that would give me back more energy. I needed to learn the basics. When I say basics, I am talking about sleeping, eating and exercise. I realize these are very basic but without these things being addressed, no amount of medication or counseling will benefit you as much as it could.

Making sure you get a good night's sleep is one of the most important things you can do in helping to stabilize when you have mental illness. Your body needs that time to recover and reset. I think in general, we completely underestimate the importance of a good night's sleep. Max takes voice lessons. His teacher told him that one of the best things he can do for his voice is to make sure he gets a full eight hours of sleep. Max notices a huge difference in warming up his voice on the days he's had eight hours of sleep versus the days he hasn't. Most of you are probably not worried about getting enough sleep so you can sing properly using good technique. I'm guessing most of you are more worried about getting through the next day without melting down or exploding. My point is if eight hours of sleep is so vital for something as small as voice technique, imagine how important it is when dealing with something as big as mental illness.

I know this sounds much simpler in theory than it is in reality. Generally speaking, dealing with mental illness significantly affects the amount and quality of your sleep. It's probably one extreme or the other. Either you're sleeping so much you can't get out of bed even after sleeping twelve hours, or you're not able to fall asleep at all because you can't get your mind to turn off and you're only able to sleep a few hours at a time. Neither one of these is a great place to be but if I had to pick between the two of these, I'd say it's much better to sleep too much and not be able to get out of bed. At least then your mind and body are getting a rest. When you operate regularly on interrupted or inadequate amounts of sleep, you are in an exhausted mental state. You will not be able to think clearly and will probably have a hard time seeing things with the proper perspective. Sleep deprivation wreaks all sorts of havoc on your body. If you don't get enough sleep you get sick more often, you get headaches and other things that could be hard to distinguish between side effects from medication and side effects from lack of sleep. You cannot afford to have your body acting up due to lack of sleep. You've got enough on your hands trying to manage medication and mental illness.

Figuring out how to get enough sleep should be the first thing on your list of priorities. If you are having trouble with your sleep schedule, either not being able to sleep or sleeping too much, talk to your doctor. Sometimes medication dosages can be adjusted so that you can get help to accommodate you getting a full night's sleep.

I have a friend who has the craziest, busiest schedule I've ever heard of. She starts at 4:30 am and works late into the night taking care of her family, multiple jobs and other responsibilities. I have no idea how she does this day after day. She is one of the hardest workers I know. Somehow she is able to push herself and continually operate like this. I remember one time asking her how in the world she manages to keep this schedule up on such a small amount of sleep. She told me once that sometimes she wishes she could be in a car accident just so she wouldn't have to do everything that's on her plate. She just wants to lay in a hospital bed and sleep. Then she would have an excuse not to be everywhere and do everything. That is nuts. After she told me that, when I would talk to her, I would offer to take naps for her. If only it worked like that. Other people may be able to function on less sleep (although I do think it will catch up to them someday), but you are not other people. You are dealing with mental illness. You cannot afford to put undue stress on your body by not getting enough sleep. You have to do everything in your power to give your body the chance to stabilize and recover so that you have the energy you need to focus on improving your situation. You are trying to thrive. Thriving is not possible on too little sleep.

I need more sleep than Adam. Sometimes it drives me nuts and I wish that I could function on less sleep and get up at 5:00 am ready to face the day. The fact is I can't. I know I need more sleep and I have to make it a top priority in my life. I take my pills at the same time every night. I go to bed at the same time every night. Sometimes I feel like a three year old because I am the only grownup I know that has to miss out on fun things with my friends because I have to go to bed on time. One year Adam's law firm had their annual attorney dinner at the Ocean Club in Scottsdale which if you know, is a VERY nice restaurant… as in bathroom attendants nice. (I never even knew a bathroom attendant existed before this.) I was so excited to go! I had been looking forward to it for weeks. When the big night came, we drove out to Scottsdale where our dinner started at 6:30 pm. Now, dinner at a nice restaurant is an event. It takes time. There are many courses to eat and time to relax in between. When 9:15 pm hit, we were just getting to the dessert menu. This was a serious dilemma because I *love* a good dessert and I knew if I had to foot the bill, I would not be going back to that restaurant anytime soon. However, I also knew that my bedtime was in forty-five minutes and we were forty-five minutes away from home. Sadly we left the restaurant. I am still a little bit bitter that I didn't get the dessert and I'm not sure when I'll get over it. But being stable is more important to me than eating dessert and I know if I get to bed late it will throw off my cycles for at least a few days, maybe even a week. That is not worth it to me. As hard as it is, I have to make bedtime a very high priority.

I don't set my alarm in the morning. I wake up when I wake up. Sometimes that's early enough to get up and get a jump start on my day. I love the mornings when my eyes pop open early and I can get in a bike ride before it gets too hot or get my chores done for the day before the rest of the house is up and going (alright I'm never up and going before Adam but he gets up at 5:00 am when the rest of the reasonable world is still sleeping). But those days are few and far between. Most days I wake up just in time to see my younger kids out the door and to give them a hug. This has been a huge source of frustration to me. Sometimes I think in my head if I were just more disciplined, I could get up at a reasonable early hour (like 6:00 am) and get going. It makes sense that my body would adjust to the new schedule. If I get up earlier, I will get tired earlier and therefore fall asleep earlier which in turn will allow me to get up earlier. Makes sense right? Except it doesn't work that way for me. I don't ever fall asleep earlier I just get less sleep. When I get up earlier and my sleep is cut short I start to melt down. The first day is usually fantastic. I'm super excited about having more day in front of me. I hate wasting the most productive morning hours sleeping. Day number two starts off good but goes downhill in the afternoon. By the evening time I am waaay too emotional over things that aren't that big of a deal. I get irritated easily. I end up sending myself to my room to protect the rest of the family from undue and unwarranted emotional overspill. If I continue on the third day, it really is a train wreck. All of my symptoms start reappearing and

I feel overwhelmed, stressed out, and completely incapable of handling my life. This is not somewhere I want to be. It is not worth it to me. If sleeping in a few extra hours helps me to be happy and have energy during the day, if it helps me to eliminate the symptoms of mental illness, that to me is a good trade off. That is why I don't set my alarm. It is what it is. Learn to work with your mental illness so you are working smarter, not harder.

In order to do this, you will probably have to do some planning the night before. Make sure that the family will be taken care of and prepare for the morning as much as possible before you go to bed. We pack lunches the night before and put backpacks by the front door. Sometimes I put cracked wheat in the crockpot to cook overnight. Sometimes I also make breakfast burritos in big batches that we keep individually wrapped in the freezer so they can be warmed up in the microwave. That way in the morning the kids already have breakfast ready without me having to get up.

The most important thing to realize here is you need to have a routine. Having a routine is what helps me stay stable. This is why I take my pills at the same time every night. It's also why I go to bed at the same time. I don't always fall asleep right away but having my body in the same routine and having quiet down time at the same time each night allows my mind to turn off and helps me relax. Even if I don't fall asleep right away, there is still value just by being in bed. My body is unwinding. I am getting rest. Sometimes this schedule interferes with my social life. I don't plan things that will keep me out late. I say no to a lot of things. I didn't used to be this strict with my sleeping schedule and routine but once I started doing it, I realized the big difference that it made in my stability. Being stable is much more important to me than having a night out with other people. I don't want to sound completely inflexible because sometimes I do choose to stay out late for a special occasion. I just have to realize that it will take me a few days to recover from that. I need to schedule down time the following day and make sure I get plenty of sleep in order to recover. It's fine for me to do that occasionally but not on a regular basis. Regularly giving up late nights and unnecessary social events is something I'm ok with. This trade-off is worth it to me. I want to thrive.

The next basic that you need to keep control over is food. Food is fuel. Food is what makes your body work and without proper nourishment, everything starts to go haywire. If you're not eating enough food regularly and eating the right kinds of food, you can feel lethargic and have no energy. You can get headaches and feel dizzy. You can have an upset stomach and be nauseated. None of these things are helpful to you when you're trying to chart side effects and figure out what symptoms are caused by your medication. You need to be very sure that the symptoms you are charting are definitely from medication if you hope to be able to fine tune the medication and work to eliminate those side effects. In order for that to happen, all other possible causes of different side effects need to be eliminated. This is especially true with food. Make sure that you are eating foods that make your body feel good and give you the most possible energy. When you eat, get the most bang for your buck. Make the calories you eat count and be smart where you're spending your calories. Don't eat empty calories that aren't going to make your body feel good. I'm sure you don't need me to tell you what healthy food is. But I will anyway. Make sure your diet is made up primarily of fresh fruits, vegetables and proteins. This is not rocket science. We've all been taught about the food pyramid from the time we were in elementary school. Food groups may be very boring to talk about and a little redundant but controlling your diet and eating healthy foods is critical to your success in managing mental illness.

I'm not talking about carrying around a food journal and scale and weighing your portions of protein, veggies and carbs. I'm simply talking about being aware of what you eat and when you eat. Eat three meals a day. Eat snacks in between. Don't ever get to the point where you're feeling sick or dizzy in any way because you haven't eaten enough food or you haven't eaten the right kinds of food. I am not a food nazi. I don't believe in extreme diets. I do believe in healthy, sustainable food choices that help your body to feel its best. My kids pack their own lunches and from the time they were little they knew they needed a fruit, a vegetable and a protein. Granted this rule came about after my daughter went to school with only cookies packed in the lunch she made for herself but still. If they pack a fruit, a vegetable and a protein they also get to pack a treat of some sort. Call it bribery but if it gets them to be aware of what they put in their bodies then I'm in.

When we first started this, the kids were unsure what a protein was. We spent a lot of time teaching them what counts as a protein. Sometimes they would get bored with their food and get stuck in a rut. We tried to be creative in thinking of things for them to take that were outside the box. Sometimes they take a typical turkey or peanut butter sandwich. Sometimes they take rice cakes with almond butter or hummus with veggies (which, by the way, I can make both almond butter and hummus in my awesome Vitamix blender that I got when poor Sam knocked his front teeth out and had to be on a liquid diet for weeks. Bummer for Sam because he had no front teeth. Happy for me because I had an excuse to buy a Vitamix). Sometimes they take a bag of almonds or turkey and cheese roll-ups for their protein. Sometimes they take chicken wraps on whole wheat tortillas. There are a lot of options for proteins if they are bored with their lunches. If you need some ideas on what to eat for your proteins, there are a lot of healthy cookbooks out there that focus on clean eating for optimum health that you can reference. Now don't stress out and feel overwhelmed about all of this because the world will not end if you pick up a pizza if you're just not up for making dinner. It will be ok. Breathe. I'm just saying be aware.

Be smart in selecting your snacks as well. Like I said, don't eat empty calories. All food is not created equal. Eat smart so you can get the most energy out of your calories that you consume. I have a few go-to snacks that I like to eat that give me a lot of energy and make my body feel good when I'm done eating them. Some of my favorites are tomatoes with avocadoes, any fruit with a handful of almonds, cottage cheese mixed with Kashi cereal (that one has a lot of protein) or greek yogurt and granola. I'm not telling you this to impress you with my eating habits and food choices because I like a juicy burger as much as the next girl. I'm just giving a few examples in case you need some ideas on different foods to try. I get that some of these foods are not as exciting or satisfying as a bag of French fries (which I have to admit, I occasionally get a craving for). Choosing and actually enjoying eating these foods was a learned behavior for me which I did only because I felt lousy. When you feel lousy, it's amazing the things you'll do to feel better again. Making good food choices helped me to feel better and have more energy which was key for me. My energy was already drained from dealing with a mental illness so I had to make sure I got the maximum energy I could out of food to try and make up some of that deficit.

I realize that learning about healthy food in theory and consuming healthy food in actuality are two different things. It takes a lot of conscious effort and planning to eat healthy foods. It's much easier to grab something fast and pre-packaged. The key is to set yourself up for success. Don't buy foods at the grocery store that don't make you feel good after eating them even if they're convenient because if they're in the house, you're going to eat them. Make preparations ahead of time so that when you need to grab something fast, you have healthy options available. One of the things I've done to make it easier for me is to precook things ahead of time so I can grab something from the fridge and just warm it up (or even eat it cold) when I'm short on time. For example, when I shop I buy lots of chicken breasts. When I get home, I bake the entire package in the oven so we always have a Tupperware full of cooked chicken to make wraps, mix with brown rice (which I also have precooked in the fridge), add to sandwiches, or salads. This also helps on the nights that I don't feel up to cooking dinner and I tell the family it's FFY (Fend For Yourself). I try to have lots of easy things to put together that will provide my family options that are healthy. This way when it is FFY I know they are still getting a good, healthy meal.

Also make sure that you are drinking enough water. You need at least eight glasses a day to keep your body hydrated. Coconut water is one of my favorite treats. Drinking a cup of coconut water hydrates your body as much as drinking a gallon of regular water. I learned this from my psychiatrist when I was having headaches that were caused by dehydration. Water is generally the only thing I drink even at meals. I think this is one of the places people flub up the most with their food intake. Sodas and even juices are a lot of calories and have a very high sugar content. Drinking soda actually makes you more dehydrated and it fills you up so you don't feel like drinking more water. This is a classic example of consuming empty calories. If you're a soda drinker my guess is you don't drink enough water for your body to stay hydrated. I'm not pointing fingers or saying shame on you because you're free to do whatever you want. If you want to continue drinking soda then by all means, be my guest. I'm just pointing out that it's essential to get enough water in your body to feel your best and drinking a lot of soda makes it harder for you to do that. Other people may be able to be more lax and looser with their diet and beverage consumption but other people are not dealing with mental illness. You have to give yourself every possible advantage for keeping your body running smoothly and feeling your best. Controlling your diet is key to doing that.

I also notice that when I eat a lot of sugar I can have dips in my moods as well so I try to keep that at a minimum (except for dark chocolate which should be at the base of the food pyramid so I think it doesn't count). When I was little, I remember the day after Halloween sitting in my room surrounded by piles of candy. My mom would tell me that I was going to get a stomachache. I never did. When she told me that she didn't feel good after eating sugar (which is why she hardly ever ate it) I thought she was a liar-face. I thought the only reason she said that was because that was what you were *supposed* to say. That's what grown-ups told kids in order to stop them from eating candy but it wasn't even true. As I've gotten older and especially after I started having mood swings, energy dips and other symptoms of mental illness, I realized that she wasn't lying to me after all. It was all true. I feel better when I don't eat sugar. Like I said before, I am not a food nazi. I occasionally like to eat sugar and will eat a good dessert but this is the exception, not the rule. Having an occasional dessert works for me because I don't feel deprived. I know if I want to eat a dessert I can, but I just have to ask myself, is this the dessert I want to spend my very small sugar budget on? Most of the time the answer is no and I skip it. But if I really do need something sweet (which we all know happens)

I'll eat a square of dark chocolate which satisfies my sweet craving with very minimal sugar intake. Maybe you're not affected by sugar as much as I am. If that's the case then you don't need to worry about all of this ranting. But might I suggest trying to cut way back on sugar just to see if it makes a difference. That way you can make the most informed decision about what types of things make your body feel its best.

Caffeine is also something that can mess with your medications. As a general rule, like I said, I don't drink soda but occasionally I will get a craving for one. A few years ago I was on my way home from the temple with a friend. She wanted to stop for a drink and it was one of those moments of craving for me so I broke down and got a Mountain Dew. It had been years since I'd had a soda with caffeine and I knew I was sensitive to caffeine so I got a small soda. I think it was twelve ounces. This was probably 8:00 pm when I drank it. I was up that night until 4:00 am the next morning. I was so wired that sleep was impossible. It took nearly a week for my cycles to return to normal and I swore off caffeine. No way am I going to take something into my body that affects my energy and sleep cycles that much. I have to keep control of as much as I can.

Also taking drugs or alcohol into your body will mess up your cycles to the point that you can't tell what's helping or whether or not your medications are even working because of the extreme side effects of the drugs or alcohol. You should never consume any type of illegal drugs or alcohol. You can't afford the luxury of not worrying about it. If you do not take them into your system, you keep control.

When you're dealing with mental illness it's so crucial to take out all of the variables possible. Am I in a bad mood because I'm tired and haven't eaten a meal or is it because my medication isn't working? This question doesn't even need to be asked if I am controlling my food. This way the only variables involved are ones that I have less control over. I have complete control over food so I need to take advantage of that and remove it from the equation. Missing meals can have a huge effect on how your medications are working. Some medications require them to be taken with food in order for them to work their best. Make sure this is something you talk to your doctor about if you feel like your medication isn't working. I notice a big difference if I've eaten an early dinner and go to bed on a near empty stomach. I feel much stronger side effects from my medications than I do if I've eaten something before taking them. Try to pay close attention to all of the outside factors if you are struggling with side effects. Think about your routine and the amount of sleep you got. Think about the food you've eaten and whether or not you're hydrated. Do everything in your power to keep all of the extra variables controlled.

Medication can make eating more complicated just like sleeping because some medications affect your appetite. Sometimes a medication can increase your appetite and sometimes medications can decrease it. Right now, my appetite is not very big. It's a chore for me to eat regularly because I'm just not hungry a lot of the time. Food doesn't taste very good to me and it's hard to choke down a meal when I already feel full. Again, keeping control over food variables is essential so even though I'm not hungry, I still make sure I eat my three meals a day and snacks in between. Feeling energized and in control is worth it.

The last basic for me is exercise. When I finally got in to see a psychiatrist, this was one of the first things he told me. He said to get out every day even if it's just for a short walk. I have to admit I was skeptical as in, "Really genius? $300.00 an hour and that's the best you've got? Pu-leeze." But I have to say he knew what he was talking about.

Growing up an athlete, I've always been very active. I started running to stay in shape and for a stress release when I was in high school and kept up the habit for years. After I had Sam, my second son, I joined a gym. Going to the gym for me to weight lift and run was something we all regularly looked forward to. Max loved it because he got to play in the kids' area with a rock climbing wall, basketball court and had other kids to play with. I loved it because I got a break from the mom thing for a little while, got to get some aggression out through intense exercise and was able to stay fit and in shape. (Sam was just a baby but I'm sure if he could have spoken, he would have told me that he loved it too because he got to coo right along with all the other babies.) Going to the gym was my way to stay sane. I still went even all through my pregnancy with Ella. I did however have to change my exercise. I started going in to false labor so the doctor said I had to stop running and weight lifting because it was too strenuous for the baby. I knew I wanted to keep exercising so I figured the best exercise for my pregnant body, the one with the least impact that wouldn't send me into false labor (again!) was swimming. I didn't really know how to swim well at that point so I took some lessons. Then when I went to the gym, I would swim laps to get in a good workout. It worked. I still got to go to the gym and no more false labor alarms.

When my symptoms started to get worse and my energy levels dropped drastically, a lot of things had to give and exercising was one of them. I was exhausted both mentally and physically. I didn't have the energy to keep up the same exercise schedule I was previously used to. I didn't want to spend all that energy exercising when I was barely getting through the days. I thought that if I exercised I would have no energy left. I thought I wouldn't be able to do anything else during the day which would not work well for me seeing as I had three kids and all. I didn't realize that exercising, even a little bit, would give me more energy back and I would be better equipped to get through my days and handle the heavy burdens in my life both mentally and physically. Turns out my psychiatrist was right. I definitely did not have the energy to exercise with the same intensity as before so I took his advice. I went out on short walks. This was a good fit during those low times because first off, I wasn't exhausted physically when I was finished like other exercise had done. I just increased my heart rate a bit and got a little sunshine at the beginning of my day. It made me feel alive. It really did start my day out on the right foot (again, no pun intended).

When I had stopped exercising I thought that exercise was on my list of 'nice to do' instead of 'must do'. I didn't realize the huge difference that little bit of exercise made for how I felt on a daily basis. I needed the endorphins to help me feel better. I needed the freedom of being outside and being able to concentrate on the exercise and forget about my problems for just a short while. It allowed me an escape. It's true you only have so much time during the day and you have to pick and choose where you're going to spend that time. If you add something in, something else must be taken away. Lay your schedule out and figure out where you can fit in some exercise. Treat it as high of a priority as you would taking your medication. It doesn't have to be something grand or even terribly intense. Start small. Start with a 20 minute walk. See how it makes you feel. See if it makes a difference in your frame of mind. It did for me. As I started feeling better and became more stable through medication, I found that my energy was slowly returning. I wanted to exercise more. I wanted the intense highs that came with pushing myself physically. I wanted to get more energy back.

When you are first starting off, or if you think you don't like to exercise, look around and find something you like to do. There are as many different ways to exercise as there are people on earth and something's got to be a good fit for you. I think one of the easiest ways to get started is to join a gym. If you've never been a big exerciser and are intimidated by this, don't worry. They have lots of group fitness classes that you can go to and stand in the back where no one will watch you. Group fitness classes are a great way to try things out. My gym has weight lifting classes, dance classes, kickboxing classes, circuit training classes, spin classes, yoga and many more. If you're still intimidated by going to a gym, you can use a personal trainer. Most gym memberships include one session with a personal trainer. This is a great way to have someone assess where you're starting from and lay out a workout plan with you specifically in mind. They will set up an exercise plan that will be good for your current level of fitness and help you to feel better. They will also walk you through each station and show you how to use the weight machines, the treadmills and other gym equipment so you can confidently find your way around a gym. If this all sounds like way too much to handle right now, don't worry. Just start with a walk.

I have found that I get tired of the same exercise over and over. I started doing triathlons for this very reason. (Well, variation was one reason but the other reason is I get really cool participant medals at the end of every race. Makes me feel like a champion!) When I get tired of my exercise and it seems like a chore instead of something I look forward to, I change it up. There are so many things you can choose from! I have a friend who takes ballet classes. I have another friend who puts headphones on and rollerblades around the neighborhood. I've gone through different exercise kicks myself. When I was younger my mentality with exercise was "No pain, no gain." I was very intense about working out and working out hard. As I've gotten older, whether it's because of dealing with mental illness or just not wanting to injure my body (after all, I have to keep this one for a really long time. I have to be nice to it), the types of exercise I enjoy has changed. Now I like to do things that are easy on my body and joints. I enjoy hot yoga. I feel like it's not only a workout for my body, but also for my mind to stay focused and in the moment. I enjoy going out on my road bike. Feeling the wind on my face, the speed of the bike and the burning in my legs gives me a serious high. Now don't get me wrong, I don't get up every morning jumping out of my skin because I'm so excited to go work out but I do think "Bike ride today. I am going to feel SO good when I'm done!" After I'm finished I take note of how I am feeling and I remember it to motivate me to go out the next day. On my mood charts I keep track of what I do for exercise and I do make notes. "Yoga – felt happy all day." It reminds me that it does matter and more importantly, that I do have some control over my cycles.

Exercising not only has the benefit of keeping your body in shape but it gives you a mental edge as well. When you are able to accomplish hard things physically, your brain registers that. It makes you feel more capable of handling challenges. It gives you confidence that you can overcome hard things. It makes you feel like you are in control of your own destiny. You are not a slave to the cycles that threaten to overtake you. This is so crucial in dealing with mental illness. You need to have the confidence and belief that you can prevail, that you will prevail. As you get feeling better and get more energy, challenge yourself. That is one of the reasons I like to do races. It keeps me dedicated to exercise knowing that I have to be ready for a race in two months but it also gives me a huge feeling of accomplishment and satisfaction knowing that I can do very hard, very challenging things. I am not broken because of mental illness. I am still in charge.

I exercise this much because I enjoy it and the intense physical and mental benefits are worth it to me even though it's difficult. It makes me feel good. You don't have to do exactly what I do. You can do whatever type of exercise makes you feel good. If all you want to do is go for a walk, then focus on that. Even that small amount of exercise will help you to feel better. Don't get stressed out thinking you have to do more than you can handle. Just commit to making some type of exercise a priority in your life so you can take more control over your cycles and feel your best.

I have a quote from Muhammad Ali (who is a three time Heavyweight World Championship boxer) that I have framed that hangs in front of my treadmill. Whenever I feel like the task in front of me is insurmountable whether it's finishing the last few minutes of my run or feeling like I can't handle the heavy weight of mental illness one more day, I read it and repeat it to myself.

"I am the greatest. I said it even before I knew that I was. Don't tell me I can't do something. Don't tell me it's impossible. Don't tell me I'm not the greatest. I'm the DOUBLE greatest."

It gives me chills just writing it down. I love that he said he was the greatest even before he knew that he was. It's okay if you're afraid of this challenge in front of you. It's okay if you're not really sure that you can do it yet. As you move forward taking each baby step at a time, you will gain more confidence in yourself and your ability to handle this very challenging thing. I have confidence in you. With each small success and each little victory you will come to realize you can overcome this and that you too are the greatest.

CHAPTER 7

THE FUNHOUSE MIRROR

• • •

Do you remember going into the fun house at a circus or amusement park and seeing the mirrors that distort your image? In one you may have a monster forehead. In the next your hips look like the size of Miami. Each mirror distorts your image in its own way but none of them accurately portray how you really look. You need a regular ol' flat mirror for that. Or an identical twin to look at. Sometimes my reality is a lot like the funhouse mirror. What I see and feel happening around me may actually be a distortion of what is really going on. This one took a long time for me to figure out and I think everybody, even those without mental illness do it to some degree. We view situations and circumstances through the lens of our own experiences. This makes sense because that's all we have to draw on, but sometimes our own experience distorts what is actually happening. Let me give you an example.

When Ella was nine she was vice president of a club that she was in with her friends. She took this very seriously and even had calendared meetings for everyone to attend. When

I asked her what they did in their club she said "Mom. We do fundraisers and we're having t-shirts made." There you go. That's what they did in their club. So one day she came home in tears and she was steaming mad about one of the girls who was, and I quote, "all up in my business." When I asked her more questions I found out that the other girl had tried to calendar a meeting about the t-shirts that were being made. The mom making them had some questions for the girls that they needed to decide on. Ella was invited to the meeting along with all the other girls. She was mad that her friend had the nerve to schedule a meeting without Ella's permission as this was solely the job of the vice president. Obviously. We talked it through some more and I asked her "Do you think she's trying to get up in your business or do you think maybe she just saw that you needed a meeting and was trying to fill a need?" All it took was that one question then she was able to see it in a different light. She changed from being mad to being glad that her friend cared about the club and was trying to help get things done.

Sometimes we don't see things clearly. We think the doctors or loved ones are trying to force us to do things to make our lives miserable. We assign people ulterior motives and think they're out to get us and doing things deliberately to make us feel bad. While there is the possibility of a rogue doctor maliciously ruining peoples' lives, the probability of that is pretty slim. The problem is our perception.

Distorted thinking is a dangerous place to be. Not being able to recognize that your thinking is distorted is even more dangerous. This is when suicide happens. If you are able to see things clearly and accurately, you will realize that no one will be better off without you. In fact the gaping hole that would be left behind would be devastating to family and friends. They would never be the same again.

Adam had a friend from high school who took his life and in the note that he left behind, he said that there was no one who cared. He had no friends or support system. This was entirely untrue. At his funeral there were so many people there who loved and cared about him that every single seat was taken and people were busting out of the building. There was standing room only. If only he could have seen accurately what other people really saw in him and felt about him. Imagine the difference that would have made.

This is what you need to learn. You need to learn how to see through the distorted thinking so you can get an accurate picture of reality. This is a fundamental life skill that will benefit you and your family forever. I don't think it's possible to sort through your perceptions and figure this out on your own. I think a counselor is vital to this and it will probably take many visits. Some people might be able to do this in weeks or months and for others it might take longer. Having a good professional counselor will help you short cut the learning curve and give you a good grasp of the proper techniques and fundamentals to help you learn to work with mental illness. They can help you see around the illness so that your mind is clear and you can focus on thriving in your life.

Since you all know I love sports, I'm going to give you a sports analogy about the importance of learning the fundamentals. John Wooden coached basketball at UCLA. His team won the NCAA national championship ten years out of twelve. Seven of those wins were consecutive. They won eighty-eight consecutive games which has never been matched. He was named a member of the Basketball Hall of Fame for being both a player and a coach. He is one of only three people to ever receive that honor. He is famous for focusing on the fundamentals. Every year when he would get his new team, his first lesson to them was how to properly put on basketball socks and shoes so they didn't get blisters. He spent an entire practice on this skill. I'm sure all of his players had been putting on their own shoes and socks for years but this was important enough to him that they all knew 100% how to do it correctly so that they didn't get blisters and it didn't affect the game.

You may think you already know how to manage your thoughts and navigate through life and you might be right. But maybe there are some fundamental skills and techniques that a counselor could teach you that will make your life easier and more manageable. Why not give it a try?

Finding a good counselor that fits your personality is essential. You need to find someone you feel comfortable with. You have to trust their opinion and appreciate the way they can help you. I've been to see several counselors and some I feel were exceptionally helpful while others were not so much. The first counseling appointment I had almost turned me off entirely. It was far from where I lived so I'd been in the car for a while and needed to use "the facilities". I entered the office and checked in. Then, knowing I had a full hour scheduled, I got a drink and went to the bathroom. The counselor then called me in his office and the conversation went something like this:

> Him: "I noticed that when you got here you got a drink and went to the bathroom. Why did you do that?"
> Me: "Because I was thirsty and I had to go to the bathroom."
> Him: "You took a lot of time doing that. Are you sure it wasn't because you were apprehensive about meeting with me and subconsciously delaying our appointment?"
> Me: "No, I'm pretty sure it's because I had to go to the bathroom."
> Silence followed by a deep, meaningful glance
> Him: "How does Mequell really feel?"
> More silence followed by a look of disbelief from me
> Him: "Where did you go? You're deep down inside."

Seriously? I can't even have a conversation with you. I refuse to talk to anyone who refers to me in third person.

The next counselor I tried was a great match for my personality. She was kind and direct and helped me make great progress in viewing myself more accurately. She did a good job teaching me the fundamentals. A key factor to look for in a counselor is someone who helps you do things differently not just someone who sympathizes with your problems and allows you to wallow in your emotional mess without offering any kind of solution. This should not be a wallowing session. This is a work session.

When you first start seeing a counselor, expect the first few visits to be filled with letting them know your back story. They will need this information to get an accurate picture of where you're at and the areas you will need to work on together. They need to have a basic understanding of what's led up to this point in your life and what some of your distorted perceptions may be. They are there to help. Once you've established a foundation with them when you leave their office, just like the doctors, you should have a list of things that you're working on before your next session. This could be anything from reading a book to working on pages in a workbook or even role playing a difficult conversation you would like to have with someone. Make sure you bring your notebook. This can be used to jot down reminders during your session and the areas that you will be working on. You can also use it during the week when you think of questions for the counselor or different areas you would like to address. It's helpful to have a road map of sorts and something to refer back to when you feel like you're stuck in a rut. If you keep a detailed notebook you can look back and see all the areas that you have improved on. It reminds you that you are accomplishing things and you can see in black and white all the areas that you have made great strides in.

One of the first things the counselor addressed with me was getting a more accurate perception of myself. I was quick to discount the good things I'd done but I never gave myself a break in the places I had screwed up. I was extremely hard on myself. I think that is one of the biggest challenges when dealing with mental illness. You only see the bad. Give yourself credit for the good things you do. See the good things you do. When things are going good, make a point to connect your actions with the good results. Sometimes I explain away the good things in my life to luck or actions of others and never take credit for the hard work I've put in but I am quick to take the blame if things go poorly. There are many examples in my life of this.

When I went back to school for the graduate prerequisites I scored really well on a chemistry test. I told Adam it was because the teacher spoon fed the information to the students so it really didn't count that I got 100%. The classes were easy since they were at a community college and really the students didn't work as hard as they did at a university. These were all of my reasons why my high score didn't count. He asked me what the class average was on this particular test and the class average was 78%. There were only 4 people in the entire class that got above a 90% yet I still felt that my good grade wasn't due to all the effort I put in or that I was smart, it was simply because the feat wasn't all that impressive to begin with. This is faulty thinking. I am fortunate to have someone who sees the good in me and tries to get me to see it as well. This was the most difficult thing I remember when working with my counselor. It was so hard to recognize and say anything good about myself. This takes constant practice even now and it still feels uncomfortable. In my head I remember Pres. Benson's[15] talk on pride and the evils of it. I think if I feel happy or

---

15   President of the church from 1985-1994

satisfied with myself then I must be prideful. This is not true. If I refuse to see areas I can improve in I could be prideful but recognizing my own hard work and good attributes is not being prideful, it is being thankful both to Heavenly Father for blessing me and myself for trying hard.

Practice positive self-talk. Be aware of what you tell yourself on a daily basis. This is a learned skill that comes from a lot of practice. No one determines how you think except for you. What you tell yourself and the things you focus on determine your reality. It doesn't matter if you have cheerleaders in every direction trying to pump you up and encourage you. If you are focusing on the negative and that is all you repeat to yourself in your head, you still won't have an accurate perception of reality. You won't be emotionally healthy. You won't be able to thrive. You need to be able to talk yourself up. Instead of focusing on the areas you fall short or your weaknesses, congratulate yourself on the areas you're doing well in. Encourage yourself for the small steps you are taking to change your thought process because it's hard work! Rewiring your brain to be uplifting and positive takes time and constant attention. When you find yourself slipping back into old habits and beating yourself up mentally, stop. Take a breath. Make a conscious decision to tell yourself something positive. Be as nice to yourself as you would to other people. One time I was telling Adam how frustrated I was with something I was working on. I was not being very nice to myself. He said "That's a harsh self-assessment. You would never say that about someone else so why would you say it to yourself?" It's true. I would never be that mean to another person. Don't be that mean to yourself.

Staying locked in on negative things is like getting stuck looking at the funhouse mirror. Certain features are exaggerated and enlarged while others are microscopic. Can you imagine if you tried to address your physical features by going off what you saw in the funhouse mirror? What if your nose looked like it took up half of your face? Would you get a nose job? That would be ridiculous to try and address fixing your physical features based on what you saw in the funhouse mirror. You are not looking at reality. You just need a new mirror. The same thing is true mentally. Get an accurate picture of where you are before you start worrying about addressing the issues. Be able to recognize that the negative things you are focusing on about yourself are not an entirely accurate representation of the whole you. Make sure you balance your view of yourself to include all of the positive and the good things you do. Change your perception. Get a new mirror.

You may need some help to do this. Sit down and write out a list of all the positive things about yourself. You can write down physical characteristics. You can write down personality traits. If you have a hard time coming up with a list, think of all the compliments that you've received from other people. Write those down. If you're still having trouble, ask someone close to you to help. If that's what you're focusing your brain on, you may be surprised to read all of the wonderful things that you've written. After you make that list, post it somewhere you'll see it every day like the bathroom mirror. When you get ready in the morning, read the list and fill your head with the positives. When you find the negatives taking over, remember your list.

The second area we worked on was changing my perspective of how I thought others viewed me. I thought that because I was so critical of myself others must view me the same way. They must only see all the areas that I'm struggling in. If I mishandled a situation I wrongly assumed that everyone involved thought I was a wreck of a person. Just like I did with myself, I discounted compliments from other people and instead held on to criticism or negative things that I heard. My perspective of how I thought other people viewed me added a tremendous weight to my already heavy burden. I felt like the people around me were judging me harshly. It's true that there were a few people who judged but it was also true that there were more people who loved. Whenever I started to feel like other people were being critical, I had a phrase that I would repeat to myself. "Everyone loves me and they're trying to help." It was amazing to me that if I repeated it enough, I would start to see where that was true. I would stop looking for signs that people were critical and start seeing all the ways that people were showing love and support.

I remember teaching Relief Society lessons and sometimes feeling like I was a terrible teacher. When Adam would ask after church how the lesson went, I would tell him it wasn't one of my finer ones. There were some areas that I did not feel went perfectly. I was certain that everyone there thought the same thing. I remember a few times specifically that I thought that and Adam said "Well that's funny because Sister So-and-So came up to me after church and told me it was one of the best lessons she's heard." I realized that I was projecting my own negative distorted thinking on to other people. Other people didn't actually think what I thought they did. Compliments that I would get from other people did not jive with my perception of the situation so I discounted them. I wouldn't listen to the ten compliments I got, instead I listened to the one negative because that's what went along with my thinking. It's true that it's hard to hear negatives and not focus on them when they come from other people but take it all in perspective. You got ten compliments and only one criticism. If you want to break that down into percentages, your positives would be in the 90th percentile. If you were taking a test that would be an A. Remember that and listen to the good. Just because one person says something negative about you does not mean that you can extrapolate that view onto everyone else. This is like in statistics taking a sample size of one. You can't draw any reasonable, accurate conclusions with a sample size of one. You'd be laughed out of academia. Do not listen to the one negative voice. Listen to the positive that comes back to you and assume everyone feels the same way. Don't unnecessarily add to your own weight. Don't get stuck in the funhouse mirror.

Sometimes when I find myself getting stuck in a mental rut, I pull out my cards. My love language is definitely words of encouragement. When I get thank you cards or nice notes from people, I keep them and they're in a special drawer in my closet. Whenever I start to feel down and feel like no one cares or understands, I pull out all the cards and read them through. It's a huge mental pick-me up for me to see all the good that others see in me. It's good for me to read letters that people cared enough to send. It reminds me to see the good and to also realize that other people see the good too.

When you are dealing with mental illness it's important to expand your circle of support. I am a private person by nature so opening up and asking for help from other people was extremely difficult for me. It's essential though to have people who understand your situation and know ways that they can help. My family is my greatest source of understanding and support. They see the situation up close and personal and they step in and help whether it's with words of encouragement or picking up the heavy load at home with running the house and taking care of the kids. The other day I was feeling overwhelmed and a little stressed out and I told Sam that I didn't want to make dinner. He said "Then don't. We know how to make food. Don't worry Mom. You've taught us well." I feel like they lift the burden with me.

It's also important to expand your circle of support outside your family. You don't need to tell everyone about your struggles with mental illness. This does not need to be public information or the first thing people know about you but it will help you if you have a few key friends outside of your family who understand and know how to help. I've been surprised a few times when I've opened up to friends and then found out that they also have a family member or close friend with this same struggle. Many times it has helped both of us to have another resource in each other who gets it and understands how to help. You can connect with people on another level if you open up.

If you're struggling, don't make other people try and guess what the issues are because you're afraid to open up and share. Just like when I shared my struggle with teaching Relief Society with the president, if other people understand the issues, they're much more willing to accommodate and look for ways to help. Don't expect other people to be mind readers. You will have to develop excellent communication skills and understand your own needs very specifically so you can ask for the help that you need. If you are struggling and need some extra help and you don't open up to the people around you that are affected, they will be forced to draw their own conclusion which may be very inaccurate and possibly hurtful to you. This is where people may be judgmental, when they don't understand. I've found that most people, once they understand the situation, are very encouraging and helpful. If they're still judgmental even after hearing the situation then that's their bag of issues. Don't worry about it. However if your struggle is putting a strain on your relationship with someone and you don't open up to them to explain why, you will have damaged relationships that will take some work to put back together. But all is not lost because relationships can be fixed. Even relationships that are very strained can be worked on and repaired with good communication and effort. Be proactive. Lead where you want the relationship to go. This is something you can learn how to do with a great counselor.

I have a few key phrases that I use at home to help facilitate good communication. The first one is "Use your words." If someone is upset and acting salty as we like to say but no one knows exactly why, I will tell them to use their words. This way the rest of the family understands exactly why they're upset, what we've done that offended them and how to avoid the same situation in the future. We can't expect people to rectify an offensive situation by guessing why we're upset if we're not willing to use our words and explain why. It's a good reminder for myself as well if I'm not feeling well to use my words and explain to the family that today is a hard day for me. My bad mood does not have anything to do with their actions and behavior. It reminds me not to take my bad mood out on the family. I need to keep my emotions in check and make sure I'm being responsible in my treatment of others and practicing good communication.

The second phrase I use is "Listen to their words." If my kids are arguing with each other and not listening to what the other person is trying to say, I remind them to listen to their words. It helps them to actively listen and understand where the person is coming from instead of just arguing to get their own point across. It helps validate each person's point of view when the other side actively listens to understand what they are trying to say. If I am feeling unheard I also say "Listen to my words." I've even used it with people outside my family when I feel pushed or backed into a corner and I am trying to say no to stay within my energy budget. Asking for other people to listen to my words has a positive dual effect of them actively listening to me and me returning the favor and really listening to what they are saying and what they feel the issues are.

The last phrase I use is "Respect my words." This means if I have given an answer to the kids, they need to respect what I am saying and not continue to push for what they want. This also works when they are teasing each other and one of them uses their words to ask the other one to stop but they continue to tease. Telling them to respect the others' words reminds them listen and take others' words seriously. Respecting someone's words means you hold them in high enough esteem that you will honor their wishes when they've asked for something. All of these things help us communicate both for me personally with my illness and my family so we have good communication and really are all on the same team. It helps us to have each others' backs.

Back when Adam and I were newly married in the beginning stages of mental illness, I had a day when I was really struggling personally. We were traveling which was always stressful for me and we were staying with some family members. That night I felt terrible. I just wanted to get to bed and regroup. Everyone was together in the family room and I just got up and left right as some more family was arriving. I was on my way upstairs and didn't even turn around to say hello. I went straight to my room. I was just trying to survive the night. One of my family members was offended that I hadn't come back to greet them and felt personally singled out and ignored. They didn't know what my struggles were. It took a long time and a lot of effort and communication to try and repair that relationship. Once we started to communicate with each other and could see the situation from the other's point of view, we were able to reconcile and move on to building a better relationship.

This is actually a fun game Adam and I play with each other. When someone is acting in a way that we think is crazy, we try to come up with an explanation that would make their behavior make sense. For instance, we'll be driving in the car and someone will zoom around us cussing and cutting us off. Adam will look at me and say "Name the situation. Go." Then I'll come up with some crazy explanation of how their great Aunt Matilda just had a heart attack on the other side of town. The neighbors can't help because they were not on friendly terms so this person is her only hope of making it to the hospital alive and they only have two minutes left to get there. It's great fun thinking up crazy situations and goes a long way in helping to see situations from someone else's point of view. The more you practice, the better you get. When we were at one of Sam's football games there was a woman on the other side of the field that was screaming and yelling for the other team and ringing her exceptionally loud cowbell nonstop. I thought it was so obnoxious! I even turned to Adam and said "I'm going to hurt that lady before this game is over." He turned to me and said "Name the situation. Go." I immediately told him that football was her favorite sport and she worked every single Saturday. Today was the first Saturday she had off all season long and she had to get all her cheering in for the whole season during this one game. Instantly my attitude toward this woman changed. We've been playing this game for so long now that whenever I come across rude or offensive behavior from someone I automatically wonder what is going on in their life that would account for their behavior.

Seeing situations from other people's point of view and helping other people understand situations from your point of view is the key to having happy, healthy relationships in your life. Don't be afraid to communicate with other people to help them see the situation from your point of view. Get the support you need by selectively sharing your situation and asking for help. Alternately, taking offense from other people especially where none was intended and keeping it to yourself is like poison. You are the only one it hurts. You already have enough on your hands dealing with mental illness. Don't take on any extra baggage hanging on to bad feelings for other people.

I was talking to my son Max the other day and he was frustrated about a situation with one of his friends. This same dynamic that was frustrating him had come up a few different times with this friend and he was exasperated trying to figure out how to change it and what he was doing to cause it. I told him "Max, don't worry about it. This dynamic is just part of your friend's bag of issues. It doesn't mean you can't be friends with him or that he's a bad person. All it means is this is an area that he struggles with. Don't take it personally or stress out over it because, even though it doesn't seem like it, it actually has nothing to do with you."

Everyone has a bag of issues they're working on. Some people are more aware of them than others but having a bag of issues does not make you a bad person. It doesn't make you a mess. All it means is you have some work to do in trying to see through the distortion and work in a particular area. Recognizing that you have a bag of issues in the first place is actually a big step. If you can recognize the distorted thinking in your bag of issues you will be ten steps ahead because you know specifically your hot spots. You are aware of the things that you may not be seeing accurately. Being aware is how you see past that funhouse mirror.

When I was on my mission I remember listening to a zone conference from my mission president. He was talking about humility. He told us that he prayed frequently that he would be humble so that he wouldn't have to be compelled because being compelled to learn anything is always very painful. That perspective has stuck with me throughout my life. If I can be aware of my weaknesses and be actively trying to work on them and improve, maybe Heavenly Father won't feel the need to painfully bring them to my attention. Since hearing my mission president, I've tried to look objectively at my life and see the areas I need to work on then go from there. It helps me keep the pride out because I am very aware of my own personal weaknesses. It also keeps me progressing and moving forward in my personal development. Working on my own bag of issues has made me a much less critical and judgmental person when I see other people struggling in their lives. Even if I notice things in their bag of issues, I don't spend much time forming opinions about them or worrying about what they need to do to address them. I am very busy addressing my own bag of issues. I don't have time to worry about anyone else's. If you find you're wasting energy and adding to your own burden by judging or criticizing other people, consider this fair warning, you are about to be painfully compelled. I suggest trying to stop this on your own. Don't waste your energy having opinions on things that aren't your responsibility. Your hands are already full.

Being able to separate yourself from your bag of issues and also from mental illness will go a long way in understanding your value as a person. You are not your illness. Mental illness is not inherently part of your character and it will not go with you into eternity. This is a temporary problem that you'll deal with in this life only. Separating yourself from your illness is critical in keeping the proper perspective. It helps you to be encouraged that you are still a valuable person. It also will help you enormously in the next major step to managing your illness. You need to be able to separate yourself from the emotions that come with the swings. You need to be able to step back and take yourself intellectually out of the emotions. You don't have to get caught up in the suicidal lows. You don't have to get caught up in the anxiety and depression or the distorted thinking. You need the ability to separate yourself from your illness. You can learn this skill from a good counselor. You can learn to recognize the distorted emotions and feelings. Instead of reacting to them you can calmly step aside in your head until your thinking is clear again because the emotions may not be tied to something you've done. Sometimes they're just part of a cycle and will correct themselves on their own if you give it some time. If you can learn how to manage this, you will be working smarter. Getting caught up in the emotions of mental illness is a huge drain and takes up a tremendous amount of energy. Stepping back and waiting to see if the emotions subside on their own as your cycles change will conserve your energy so you can use it in smarter ways.

Let me give you an example to illustrate what I'm talking about. Sometimes when I am down I get a huge anxiety pit in my stomach. It's hard to describe to people who haven't felt it on their own but the closest feeling I can describe it by is the feeling that you get when you've sinned or done something terribly wrong. Having that pit of despair and the guilt that comes with it is a terrible thing to feel. When I first started feeling this, I was convinced it was because of something I had done. I would rack my brain trying to figure out what terrible sin I'd committed or offensive thing I had done that would explain this awful feeling.

I remember one time when a ward member had gone through a tragedy in their family. Whenever I saw them over the next few weeks, I would ask how they were doing. A few weeks later, the Relief Society president got up and wanted to thank everyone for help with meals and other needs for the family. Then she said that while they were grateful for everyone's concern, it was not something they wanted to talk about on an ongoing basis. They were doing fine and trying to move on. I felt like she was speaking directly to me. I had been doing the very thing she was respectfully asking us to stop doing. I just *knew* that the family had asked the Relief Society president to announce that so I would stop talking to them about it. I felt terrible. I obsessed for days and had an awful pit in my stomach. I was having trouble eating and sleeping. I couldn't think about anything else other than what a terrible faux pas I had made. I finally decided that I had to do something to make it better. So I wrote an apology letter to the wife for intruding on their family and not giving them the privacy they desired. After I sent the letter, I got an email back from a very confused lady asking if I had sent the letter to them by mistake. She had no idea what I was talking about and said they had always felt nothing but love and concern from me. Well, try explaining that away. "Don't mind me, I've just been obsessing for days over a problem that never really existed." That was definitely a day that I felt like I needed a counselor.

This is what I'm talking about though. I felt down. I felt terrible. It thought it must have been something I had done. I thought there was something I could pinpoint in my actions that explained to me the bad feeling even though it was not accurate. It took years of practice to sort through the distortions in my thinking to be able to step back and not get caught up in the emotions. If you are feeling bad, don't jump to conclusions. Don't react to people or situations quickly. Sometimes it's best to sit and let them marinate for a while. If you've given it a week or so and you still feel like this is an issue that needs to be addressed, go ahead and address it then. You'll have a better handle on your emotions and hopefully you will have used that time to articulate specifically what the issue is so when you communicate with someone about it, you can be better understood.

When I am down I stay home and don't answer my phone. Or my door. Seriously. The reason for this is I know I shouldn't be talking to people when my mind is distorting reality. It's probably not so much that I shouldn't be talking to people as much as I need to be aware that my interpretation of the conversation could be slightly off. I get offended easily and tend to hear only the negative things. Problems seem larger than they are when I'm up. Sometimes after a few days I realize the problems I was obsessing about aren't even real. I twisted everything in my head to make sense out of how I was feeling.

When you're down, you feel *so* bad inside. It only makes sense to try to find a reason for the terrible feeling. Instinctively, you look at everything going on around you and try to figure out why you feel so bad. This is where the distorted thinking comes in to play. Sometimes you feel bad *just* because you're down. That's it. It's not because of anything you've said or done or anything that's been said or done to you. It's just because you're down. Soon you will feel better and whatever it is that you've attributed this terrible feeling to will neutralize in your head and you'll see it really wasn't (fill in the blank) after all. It was just a cycle.

Being able to intellectually separate yourself from the emotions will also help you feel more in control and less likely to panic. The key to thriving in your life with mental illness is having the ability to see things clearly. If you can understand that this bad feeling is part of a cycle of your illness, you can save yourself a lot of worry, stress and energy. Work smarter.

If you find yourself stuck in a cycle where you feel like everything is a disaster and nothing will get better, make a list. This can be an actual list or it can be something you just name off in your head or talk about with a loved one. When I find myself down and fixated or overwhelmed by all the things that are going wrong, Adam will ask me what is going right. Then I will go through and list all the things that are going well. Sometimes they are very small things like I got a good night's sleep or one of the kids did an act of service without being asked. If you can learn to focus on the good and be able to see the good in any situation, you will be better able to keep from being stuck in the funhouse mirror.

A good counselor will be able to teach you techniques to keep a clear perspective. They will be able to teach you fundamental skills so you can see more clearly and accurately the things going on around you. They will be able to teach you how to handle and manage relationships so you have the greatest chance for success in getting the support you need. You don't need to see a counselor forever. Once you have these tools and have enough practice in doing this, you can venture out on your own. The goal is for you to be able to see things clearly and have the proper perspective by yourself. It will still help if you have someone to talk you through issues and make sure you're thinking is not distorted. This can be a great opportunity to bring you closer to your spouse, parent or friend. When I talk through things with Adam and I am wondering if I'm seeing things clearly, he has a very nice way of saying "This problem might actually be you. I don't think your perception is what's really going on." I am a lot better at this than I used to be but it still takes work. Fortunately I have years ahead of me to continue to work on this skill. Aren't I lucky?

CHAPTER 8

DON'T PULL YOUR HAIR OUT

(How to make Parenting Work with Mental Illness)

● ● ●

WHY, MIGHT YOU ASK, AM I writing a chapter on parenting in a book about mental illness? What do they even have to do with each other? The answer is mental illness changes the way you operate in your entire life and that includes parenting if you have children. If you have the proper perspective and can work with your illness, you will find that your strengths will be magnified and your weaknesses or limitations will be minimized. Bottom line, you will be a super awesome mom operating at maximum efficiency. Notice how I said maximum efficiency not maximum speed. Maximum efficiency means you are working smarter. There are no energy leaks anywhere and all of your efforts are concentrated and effective. This is a fabulous way to parent and guess what the best part is? I feel great. I am not overwhelmed, overstressed or overburdened by the number of things that need to be done as a parent (moooost of the time and then if I am, I take a day off). I prioritize (remember your budget?) and pick the most important things and then I don't worry about the rest.

I didn't always have this perspective on parenting. This is an area that can cause tremendous amounts of guilt and feelings of failure. Trust me, I have felt my share of these emotions about parenting. I grew up with a super-mom in every sense of the word. She was up very early before the rest of the family every day cleaning and cooking. We always had a big breakfast that she made (with syrup from scratch!). I always remember our dishes being done, floors being scrubbed, windows being washed (by mom, of course). She grew a garden and bottled fruits and vegetables that she had grown. She even bottled grape juice with grapes from our own vine. She had very demanding church callings that would take up many hours each week. She was the PTA president at the school. My brothers and I were also in club gymnastics practicing six days a week. She would run us back and forth to the gym which was twenty minutes away making four to six trips each day because of our varying workout times. She was always the last one to bed working on sewing projects and other things around the house. She had endless energy day after day. In short, I had very high standards and expectations of what I thought a good mom was. I didn't believe there was any other way to be a good mom.

After I had my own kids, I tried to do all of these things. I wanted to be a good mom for them. I wanted to do a good job and gave my all in doing this. It quickly became apparent that this was not something I could keep up (see previous chapter i.e. suicide). I felt like a failure, a big fat F. Every time I went to church and heard lessons on everything I should be doing as a mother I felt like a failure. Every time I went to school and saw plaques on the wall of parent volunteers of the month I felt like a failure. Every time I went to parent teacher conference and heard all the things I should be doing to help my kids excel more in school I felt like a failure. Worst of all, my kids had to take care of themselves. I felt so guilty for the terrible mother I thought I was. But then something happened -- slowly, I began to see how much my kids were growing. I began to see how responsible and independent they were becoming and I connected this letting them do things for themselves. They were growing because I was giving them opportunities to do so. I shifted my thinking from believing I needed to do it all to be a great mom to teaching my kids how to do it themselves to be a great mom. I fell into this parenting style quite by accident simply because I couldn't do it any other way. Now I've realized this has been a huge blessing to my kids. If I simply take time to teach, I am the best parent they could possibly have. I know this now and I have complete confidence in my ability as a mom. Now I parent this way on purpose. Even when I have more energy, I don't deviate from this parenting style. I believe in my heart of hearts that this is the best possible thing I can do for my kids. I prioritize what I need to teach them and what needs to get done then I don't worry about the rest.

The way I manage this is by choosing my priorities wisely, then spreading the wealth. I get lots of help from my kids and from my husband when the home and family need more attention. Now when I say this, I am not just transferring everything that needs to be done and shoveling it on to them. I still am prioritizing with everyone addressing only the most important things (which means that some things aren't getting done).

Let me give you an example. Dinner time is generally a stressful time of day. After the kids get home from school, the house sort of looks like a bomb went off and backpacks threw up all over my kitchen. I like a clean house and it makes me feel good when things are organized so generally speaking, this makes me grumpy. However, I remember that having a perfectly clean house after school is not my number one priority. My priorities after school are talking to my kids (which I allot significant time for) and attending games or activities they are participating in. Those are my top priorities. This means that making dinner is on the second tier of priorities. Are you wondering how I manage this? Let me introduce you to my good friend cold cereal. Or scrambled eggs which take five minutes to make. Or baked potatoes that I can have my kids put in the oven. You get the idea. This also means that cleaning my house is down to the third tier of priorities which means it probably isn't going to get done today. But not to worry, tomorrow morning cleaning the house is my top priority so I know it will get done then. This gives me the freedom not to worry about it and spend any energy stressing that my house is messy. It is on my list and I know it will get done tomorrow.

If it is a particularly hectic day and I am gone attending activities for kids, I enlist the help of the family. When I get home (late and frazzled) I announce that tonight dinner is F.F.Y. (Fend For Yourself). Next I enlist the help of hubby by saying "Ella had this issue come up at school today and I need you to talk to her about how to best handle the situation." Then I go and de-stress knowing that both top priorities have been taken care of and everything else can wait until tomorrow.

The important point here is I don't do everything. Some things are left undone. I don't beat myself up for this. I don't compare myself to other moms who may do more things for their kids. This is another time when you may think there's only one way to be a mom.

When I was in sacrament meeting[16] last Mother's Day, I was listening to a talk from one of the youth in our ward. He was saying how grateful he was for his mom and all the things she did for him like making his bed in the morning, making his lunch, doing his laundry, making his meals, etc. My son leaned over and said "I love my mom because she doesn't do any of those things. She lets me do them myself." It's true that my kids do a lot of things for themselves but that is because of my perspective on parenting and how I run my family.

My number one goal as a parent is to have my kids ready for the world. I want them to be responsible for their own behavior and choices and be able to think through consequences to help them make the best choice possible. I want them to understand that no one is responsible for their lives except themselves. I want them to feel empowered that they are in charge of their own lives and are confident in their ability to handle life. I want to equip them with all the tools and skills necessary

---

16 Sacrament meeting is the main worship service in the church. Church members are occassionally asked by leaders to prepare a talk to give to the congregation.

so they are ready to go out on their own. I want them to know how to cook, clean, do the laundry and wisely manage their time and financial resources. Having this mindset changes the way I operate as a parent. This means that instead of doing things for my kids, I focus on teaching them to do things for themselves. Don't misunderstand me in thinking that my kids are left high and dry with no one to show them the way. That is my job as the mom. I teach them how to handle things then step back and let them handle it.

Like I said earlier, my kids were responsible for making their own lunches from the time my daughter was in kindergarten. I had to oversee a lot of this process. We would pack lunches the night before because packing their own lunches took forever! It would have been so much faster and easier for me to do it myself but I kept reminding myself that the goal was not speed and efficiency or even having it done the best it could possibly be done. The goal was to teach them how to take care of themselves. I would have to be in the kitchen watching them and directing them what to do next which is actually quite difficult to do. My natural inclination was to grab whatever they were struggling with and do it for them because it was so much simpler. They would also have me or Adam check their lunches when they were finished to make sure they had packed the mandatory fruit, vegetable and protein so they could get their treat. Now making your own lunch in kindergarten is a big thing! In order to make it easier for them, I would cut up fruits and vegetables and have them in the fridge. Sometimes if I had lots of energy, I would even separate them into snack bags so all they had to do was grab a veggie bag and throw it in their lunch instead of having to pack it all themselves. This way I could help but the over-all responsibility of having their lunch packed was still up to them. Sometimes I felt like a really mean mom making them do this but I knew this was the best way for our family to make things run smoothly when I wasn't feeling well and couldn't do this for them. This is why I helped when I could when I had the extra energy. I oversaw them and made sure they were ready to walk out the front door before they went to bed so all they had to do in the morning was get themselves ready, clean their rooms and get breakfast.

I carried this same philosophy through with teaching the kids to cook breakfast from a very young age. When my oldest son Max was in the second grade, I was going through a medica-tion change and during the change, I was sleeping about fourteen hours a night. Fortunately, he knew how to take care of things. He would get up, get ready for school, cook scrambled eggs for himself and the younger kids who were three and four, then put on a movie for them before getting himself out the door with all his schoolwork, lunch, etc in enough time for the bus. When my medication finally wore off and I was able to wake up, the house was still running smoothly and things had been taken care of. This is exactly why it is so important to teach the kids how to do things for themselves rather than be up trying to do it all myself. Sometimes I am out of commission and cannot do these basic things. However, when this happens, there is no crisis at the house because everyone knows what to do.

When my daughter was in third grade, she was a pro at packing her lunch and taking care of herself. She came home from school one afternoon and told me how bad she felt for her friend. I asked her why and she said her poor friend didn't know how to pack her own lunch or make waffles or even do her own laundry. Her mom did it for her! Ella felt so big that she got to do this for herself. See how great it is to empower our kids with confidence? There's no reason to feel guilty because we are not doing everything for them. They love the fact that we trust them enough to do things on their own.

The kids were also responsible to remember to bring their own lunch, homework and other items needed for school. The night before, we would pack lunches and get backpacks by the front door. They would put in everything they needed for school the next day. If they forgot their lunch, I would not bring it to them at school. I knew that I was teaching them to be responsible for their own things and if I rescued them by continuing to bring things they had forgotten, I would curtail the learning curve and they would not learn responsibility. I knew they would not die if they went without lunch at school. They would be very hungry when they got home, but painful consequences are how we learn so I knew they would be much more likely to remember their lunch if they had to go without. This was another thing that was really hard for me to do. I felt like a jerk when my daughter called me in tears to please bring her homework to school. The school was right down the street and honestly it would have taken me ten minutes to do it. I had to give myself pep talks all the time about my goal of teaching them to be responsible for their own things. Remembering to bring their own homework to school is something that they are definitely capable of even in elementary school. Sometimes they would get a sad consequence of missing recess if they didn't have their homework. Sometimes they would get another sheet and try to redo the assignment before the teacher asked for it to be handed in. One time my daughter convinced her teacher to let her run home during lunch recess and bring her homework back. The point is they got creative in figuring out how to find solutions to their own problems. I just had to stay out of the way and let them learn.

My kids are now in junior high and high school. They are all much better at remembering their needed items. Occasionally I will still get a phone call if they have forgotten something. Like I said previously, as a general rule I sympathize with them on the phone and ask them how they're going to handle the missing homework with their teacher. However, if I have lots of energy that day, and it has been a very long time since they have forgotten something, I may barter with them. I understand that people are human and sometimes we forget things. I may bring the needed item to school but then I ask what they will do to make it up to me? How will you give me back the energy I'm going to spend bringing this to you? Sometimes the barter is cleaning the bathroom or vacuuming the stairs. If they desperately need the item and are willing to do something for me, I am much happier about interrupting my day to help them. Sometimes though, what they have to do in return is not worth it to them. The last time my daughter called needing her volleyball jersey that she had forgotten on the laundry room counter, I offered to bring it if she would clean the baseboards. She agreed then five minutes later I got a phone call from her. She said, "Never mind. I've found an extra jersey and I just wanted to make sure you haven't left because I don't want to wash the baseboards." Like I said, when it's up to them, they get creative in figuring out different solutions to their problems.

It's surprising how much our kids can be responsible for if we sit back and let them handle it. It's also surprising the solutions they will come up with when they know no one is stepping in to rescue them. The one thing that I have to remember is that it is ok if they come up with a different solution than what I would have done. There is more than one way to solve a problem and if I am going to empower them to handle their own situations, I need to give them the freedom to solve it in their own way.

A perfect example of this is Sam and his church pants. When Sam was four years old he wanted to wear Max's old church pants to church instead of his own. Max was significantly taller than Sam so the church pants were about six inches too long which was a problem. I told him he'd just have to wait until he grew a little more so Max's pants would not be too long on him. I went downstairs to finish getting ready for church and pretty soon Sam came down wearing Max's old church pants. I was in the kitchen and he was behind the counter so I couldn't see all the way to the floor. I asked him why he was wearing the pants and he said that I told him they were too long so he fixed them. I walked around from the counter and sure enough, the pants were no longer too long. One of the legs had been jaggedly cut off mid-shin and the other was rolled up and set in place with a glue gun. Not exactly what I had in mind, but mission accomplished. The pants weren't too long anymore. Problem solved. In case you're wondering, he did wear the pants to church that day.

Another area that was very hard for me was birthdays. Generally speaking, large social gatherings drain a lot of my energy. I very rarely attend them and I almost never host them. This was an issue with my kids because they wanted to have birthday parties. I would look around at the parties that they were invited to and it seemed that each one was bigger and more elaborate than the next. There was no way I could compete with that. I was exhausted and nearly in the fetal position just thinking about them. I had neither the energy nor the money that I wanted to commit to planning a birthday party like that. So I decided how much time and money I was willing to commit and then told the kids they would be getting a set amount of money for their birthdays. They could use this money however they wanted. They could use it all to buy a present for themselves. I could take them out to lunch and spend the afternoon with them. They could put some in their savings account where we would match it and use the rest to buy something smaller. Or if they wanted a party, they could use that money for a party. They would be in charge of everything. They had to make the invitations, plan the activities and budget for everything that would be needed. They got very good at stretching their dollars by making their own cakes, making their decorations or repurposing various things we had around the house. They shopped for deals for things they needed to purchase. Some years they chose parties, other years they chose to go shopping with me and some years they saved a portion and kept the rest on hand so they would have money when their friends wanted to do things. Their parties were not the same as other kids' parties but they were still creative and fun because no adult would think of doing the things that they planned.

Last year after Sam handed out his homemade invitations (that very much looked like they were entirely made by a thirteen year old boy), I got a call from another mother asking if this party was for real because it definitely looked like no adult was involved. I did feel a little like a schmuck at first but then I remembered: I'm not parenting this way so I look good to other parents. I am parenting this way because it helps me stay within my energy budget and gives my kids opportunities to grow. This area that initially caused a lot of guilt and stress for me turned out to be a terrific way to teach the kids about the value of a dollar and how to prioritize financially and budget their money. Now when their birthdays come around, I pat myself on the back for being brilliant enough to figure out a way to make this work for both them and for me.

Something that's important to remember as a parent is you teach people how to treat you. This includes your kids. You are the one who dictates what is and what isn't ok for them to say or do. If you set a rule or ask for something to be done, mean it and follow through with the consequence. This takes a lot of moxy and confidence in yourself as a parent. If you feel wishy-washy about yourself and feel guilty because you don't believe you're doing a good job or you are a sub-par parent because you are dealing with mental illness, you're not going to make it. Don't let anyone make you feel inferior or less in any way because you have mental illness. Don't believe that garbage yourself. If you're feeling like that, pick yourself up, shake yourself off and repeat to yourself "I'm good enough. I'm smart enough. And doggone it, people like me." If you grew up in the 80's and watched Saturday Night Live, you'll appreciate this Stuart Smalley reference. If you don't know what I'm talking about, it's still a good mantra (and you should look it up on YouTube).

Seriously though, you have to believe deep down that you are a good parent. Look at all the things you're doing well and don't beat yourself up for the things you fall short on. Understand that having limitations as a parent does not make you a bad one. In fact I believe having bipolar has made me a better parent. I don't get wrapped up worrying about trying to do everything. I know I can't so I just decide what the very most important things are for me to teach and forget about the rest. You are a great parent because you are trying. Grab a dose of confidence and march forward with your head held high knowing you're doing the best you can.

A few years ago when my kids were all in elementary school, I was taking some pre-requisites for a graduate program so I was in class all day. One day when I got home after classes, the kitchen was a mess. Now I left it that morning sparkling clean so you can imagine my dissatisfaction with the situation. After further inspection (and finding their note), I realized all the kids had come home from school and made themselves a snack then gone to play at their friends' houses. Well I am not a maid. I expect them to clean up after themselves and this is widely known in my home. I got in my car, drove around and picked all of them up from their friends' houses and brought them home to clean up the kitchen. I did this because I know everyone has to pitch in to keep our house running. Everyone has a responsibility to keep it clean. Everyone contributes to help our home run smoothly. This was another situation that took a lot more effort for me to teach them to follow the rule of cleaning up after themselves than it would have for me to just clean the mess up myself. However I knew that I was setting a precedent for the future. If I let them get away with not cleaning up and only required it sometimes, when I am out of commission and can't enforce the rule, it will not get done. I need the rules to be enforced even if I am not standing there to do it myself. By taking the extra time to impress upon them the need to follow the rules always, I am setting myself up for future success. I know the home will still run without me as long as everyone else is on board.

One of the things that has helped me the most in having our home run smoothly and the kids learning is to have systems in place and have very clear and defined expectations as well as clear consequences if expectations are not met. Let me explain this by telling you about our laundry system. Laundry is something that can get very overwhelming with a family. It is never done and I used to feel stressed out all the time by the growing pile of laundry that never seemed to end. I decided that I would implement a new policy by doing laundry on Mondays. I would devote the entire day Monday to washing, drying, and folding all of the clothes. This solved my problem of always feeling stressed out about the laundry not being done. I could have an entire laundry room piled waist high but never have to worry about it because I know that the laundry will get done on Monday. I have a time set aside for it. It is on my list. Reading what you have about my parenting philosophies so far, you can probably already guess that my kids were taught how to do laundry at a very young age. Early elementary school is when I thought they were ready to do it on their own which they did during the summers. However, even when they were in preschool, they still helped. They had pre-stain treatments in their rooms by the laundry baskets. When they took their clothes off, we would check for spots and I would have them spray the treatment on the spots so while the clothes sat waiting to get done, the spots weren't setting in and they were learning how to do the laundry.

Since I require a lot from them at home during the school year (like making their own lunches and being responsible to get themselves ready and remember practices, homework, etc), I do their laundry for them. But we still have rules. My first laundry rule is I will wash whatever is pre-sorted in the laundry room Monday morning then fold it and stack it outside the laundry room in the hallway. They have to bring their laundry baskets in, sort their clothes into the correct piles, make sure the spots have been pre-treated and have them turned right side out in order for me to do it for them. They are also responsible for putting their own laundry away. If their clothes are inside out, I will take them back to the kids' bedrooms and leave them on the floor for them to finish on their own. If they forget to bring their clothes in, they are responsible for washing their own clothes that week. They may not just skip that week and sort it for me the next Monday. That doubles my laundry load and I cannot get it done. If they forget to bring their clothes in, they don't get washed for them. End of story. If they need things washed during the week like sports uniforms or a favorite outfit, they are responsible to do that on their own. I only do laundry on Mondays.

I am very careful in guarding my Monday laundry day. Since I set it up this way, I have to make sure the laundry gets done on that day. This means I spend most of my day doing the laundry. I don't set doctor appointments, I don't run errands, I don't set visiting teaching appointments, I don't go to lunch with friends because that is the day I do laundry. My friends all know this and it's a source of humor for some of them because I guard that day as sacred. I am never available to anyone on Mondays.

This system is very clear. Everyone knows the rules. Everyone knows the consequences. Everyone is equipped to handle those consequences. This is another situation that demonstrates that I teach my kids how to treat me. I do not nag them, yell at them or get frustrated if they don't get their clothes sorted Monday mornings. I'm fine either way. I'm fine doing the laundry for them but I am equally fine having them wash their own clothes later in the week. It has taken away all of the stress and frustration I used to feel when handling the family's laundry. The reason I set this system up was to be able to take care of our family's laundry needs without overspending my energy budget. I have set the limits as to how much time and energy I have to put towards the laundry. Before setting the system up, I would have more demands placed on me than what I was able or willing to do. I would feel bad and do more laundry anyway which would put me in the "overdrawn" category of my energy budget. When other people spend my time or energy I get agitated and I found I was getting very upset and resentful about the amount of time it took me to do the laundry. No matter how much I did, people still needed more. That is not a good way for me to operate. Since setting this up, I know exactly how much time and energy I will be spending doing laundry. I am happy to do it because I know no one will be pushing me to do more than I can. I figured out what I am able to commit to then made arrangements and put systems in place for the rest of it to get taken care of.

This is what works for me. I am not saying this system will work for everyone. I am simply giving an example to demonstrate principles of ways that I can parent and take care of responsibilities at home while still taking good care of myself. That is what I want you to get out of this. You have to take care of yourself. Understand how much time and energy you have to give and act accordingly. I know there are responsibilities that need to get done but if you are creative and can think outside the box, you might find ways that will meet your needs and still have your family taken care of too.

Don't worry if your home doesn't run "perfectly" or if you have to do things differently than the ideal. The only thing that matters is you are addressing your priorities in a way that fits for you and your family. In church, I hear all the time about the importance of family scripture study and family prayer. I agree that these things are important and high priorities. Traditionally I hear of this being done early in the morning before everyone leaves for school to make sure they get sent out in the world on a good spiritual note. Max, who is in high school, leaves at 6:00 in the morning because he has "A" hour. This means that our family would need to wake up by 5:45 am to do morning scripture study together. My other kids don't leave until 8:15 am so this doesn't work well for our family. We decided that night time scripture study and family prayer fits our family better. Right before bed, we gather, read and pray. Some nights we're not home until late or everyone isn't there. Some nights we miss but we do the best we can.

In the morning, I still want to send the kids out the door with a spiritual thought. We've tried different ways to accomplish this. I tried waking up and coming downstairs to have a devotional with Max before he leaves. One problem though: my medication does not wear off that early in the morning. I've tried to get up before the medication wears off and I end up staggering around and falling into walls and furniture. This is not an exaggeration. It is entirely true.

One day I tried getting up and I fell down and hit my head on the armoire in my room and ended up with a huge knot. The devotional did not get read that morning. So then I decided I would stay safely in bed and have Max come in to my room for me to read a spiritual thought to him. The first day we tried this, it was very apparent that it would not work. My brain did not function. It took me forever to try and read! I could see the words but I could not make sense of them at all. Finally Max just took the book and read it out loud himself. That is where we ended up settling. Max comes into my room right before he leaves, wakes me up, reads out loud a spiritual thought to himself, marks the book where he read and hugs me goodbye. Later that morning I'll read the same devotional to the other kids before they leave. There are a lot of mornings I have no recollection of our devotional even after reading it to the younger kids. Sometimes I think "this sounds vaguely familiar" but sometimes I don't recognize any of it. I'll ask Max after school why he didn't come in and read with me and he always tells me "Mom, I did." Like I said, my brain does not function well that early in the morning. The point is we've found something that fits our family to accomplish the highest priorities even though it's in a different way than anyone else I know. I'm not recommending this to anyone. I'm just telling you how I've gotten creative to make it work for me.

Scripture study with my husband is accomplished with the same creativity. He has a long commute to work. He also works from home for the first few hours of the day so he misses most of the traffic. After the younger kids get out the door, he leaves for work. He calls me on the phone and we spend forty-five minutes reading the lessons for Sunday and having gospel discussions. It's not the ideal scripture study and I'm sure there are more effective ways to do it. But this is what works for our family. Don't worry if what you're doing is not the ideal way. Even though we do morning devotionals and family scripture study and prayer, I definitely don't want anyone filming us while we're doing it for everyone else to watch. Make sense? I think sometimes we misunderstand and think obedience is rigidity. This thinking is wrong. The principle is what we need to understand. We have a lot of freedom to figure out how to live those principles in ways that work for us personally. It doesn't matter what we look like compared to other people or other families.

It has been very hard for me to stop worrying about appearances. It doesn't matter how I look to other people. It also doesn't matter how my kids look to other people. The only thing that matters is we are doing what works for our family. Our family is learning and growing together and thriving. Sometimes we look a little messy during the learning process but that is something that I have to be ok with. Be ok with living your life in a way that works for you but also be ok with not worrying about superficial appearances.

Letting the kids pick out their own clothes and do their own hair was painful and hard for me. I like to dress them up and make them look nice. When Ella was little, she always had cute hair with bows and matching jewelry. My favorite part of the morning was doing something creative with her hair. I would try different braiding techniques or ideas I'd thought up or look up sites on the internet to find something pretty. I hate to say it but this was an area that I didn't want to give up control over. When Ella told me in the first grade that she wanted to do her own hair, I tried to talk her out of it. (I still can't believe I did that myself!) But Ella is just as determined as I am so she was not going to back off of getting to do her own hair. I had to step back and let her look like an orphan child that nobody loved (at least in my mind that's how she looked). My compromise was that I still got to do her hair on Sundays so I knew she would look nice at church. Sending her off to school though with hair that looked like a six year old did it was not my favorite stage. However, that was how Ella learned to do her own hair and that is an important skill for kids to have. Now she's really good at doing hair and can do all sorts of fancy braids, twists and buns. It is also a relatively pain free lesson as the worst thing that can happen is they have bad looking hair. Really not a big deal in the grand scheme of things.

A little while ago we were all sitting around the table looking at pictures from when the kids were younger. Max pulled out a picture from middle school and said "What?! You let me go out of the house with my hair looking like that? Why didn't you tell me??? I can't look anyone in the eye who ever saw me like that!" I just had to laugh. I told him "Because that's how you liked to wear your hair." He made me promise that I would tell him if he ever had bad ideas about how to do his hair in the future. The point is, let the kids control things that aren't a big deal. It gives them practice being independent and making choices for themselves. Maybe you're not a fan of their clothing style but as long as they're not dressing inappropriately, who cares? You're not the one wearing it.

I went shopping with Max after he started high school. He was picking out different clothes at the store and asking me how I liked them. He found a pair of shorts that he loved. He was so excited about them! He asked me how I liked them and I told him they weren't my personal favorite. He was very put out and demanded to know why. I told him I just didn't. No particular reason. He started to argue with me about why they were such awesome shorts and I told him "Max, if you like them then get them. Who cares if I don't have the same taste in clothes. I wear things that you don't like. If they're you're favorite then you should get them." He ended up getting the shorts and it turns out no one in the family liked them either. Every time he would start to get huffy about people not liking his shorts I would remind him "They're you're shorts. Everyone doesn't have to like them for you to enjoy wearing them."

This is definitely a learned skill. I naturally want my kids to dress and do their hair in a way that I like. As long as it's not inappropriate in any way though, it's important to let them choose and have control over their own choices. The more practice they have making choices over little things, the better prepared they will be to make choices over big things. They will be able to think through the consequences in their heads and make an informed decision. Letting them choose their own clothes and hairstyle is something they can be in charge of. It doesn't always have to be my way. There is more than one way to do something and realizing that my preference isn't the only right way is an important principle to understand as a parent in trying to raise independent, responsible children.

I had an interesting talk with Max the other day after school. As I said previously, talking to my kids after school is a top priority and I spend a lot of time doing it. When they come home, I talk to them about their day. I ask about their friends and what happened in each of their classes. Sometimes they're in really chatty moods and we'll talk for an hour. Sometimes they're not and the conversation is very short. When that happens, I follow them around the house from room to room. Not a joke. I really do this. I'll follow Max into the living room where he practices guitar and I'll sit there and listen. Sometimes he'll practice for a few minutes and then put the guitar down and talk to me some more. Sometimes I just listen to him practice. Most of the time, I end up having good conversations with my kids and I find out what's going on in their world. The point is though, I don't press them to talk to me. I just make myself available and most of the time, the talk comes naturally. I love spending this time talking to my kids but it does take a long time to facilitate.

During one of my conversations with Max a few days ago, he was telling me about some of his friends and their parents. I was asking him questions about which parents were the easiest to talk to and which ones he liked the most. When my kids' friends come over to the house I also spend time talking to them. I ask them about what sports or activities they're doing and how the team is. I ask them about their classes and teachers. I ask them all sorts of things. This is another way for me to find out what's going on in my kids' lives. It's also a good gauge when I'm wondering if their friends are helping them make good choices or hindering them in making good choices. You can get a good feel for them just by talking and asking questions. While Max and I were talking, he was telling me about one of his friends that has very strict and extremely involved parents. Max was telling me how micromanaged (he felt) his friend was. He told me "That's one thing I like about you. You don't tell me what to do very often but when you do, I always know I should do it." Giving them power to make choices over things that don't matter gives us more clout when we're instructing them on the important things.

I think my number one job as a parent is to be a counselor for my kids. When they come home and tell me about their problems with friends or teachers, I always try to sympathize and express my understanding for how hard that situation is. Then I ask them what they're going to do about it. I never take ownership of their problems. I never jump in and try to solve the situation for them. Their problems are their own and they can solve them on their own too. Many times if they don't know what they're going to do I'll ask "Do you need some ideas?" Then I'll come up with a couple different things they might try to resolve the situation. Sometimes the kids will say that they don't want any ideas so then I keep my mouth shut. I don't tell them what I think they should do. I say nothing which is really, really hard because many times I feel like "Oh, oh, I know this one!" but I have to respect their words so I don't offer my solution. I let them figure it out. After a few days I'll follow up with them and ask them how their problem is going. Sometimes it resolved itself on its' own. Sometimes they decide not to do anything about it and just live with it. Sometimes they addressed it and it went well. Sometimes they addressed it and it didn't go well. I try to ask them how they felt it went and if they would do the same thing again. If not, what would they do differently. This helps them come to their own conclusions about things they've learned. Sticky situations for our kids can be great learning opportunities if we let them think for themselves.

This is another way that helps me manage my time and energy budget in parenting. I do not have either the time, energy or even desire to jump in and try and solve every problem that comes along. If I do that I burn out and don't have the energy left to take care of myself and my family. Becoming overly involved and trying to jump in and solve their problems with teachers, friends or any number of other thing are big drains on my energy budget. By handling the problems that my kids encounter the way I do, I reserve my energy for something that has the most impact which is teaching them to solve their own problems. The next time a similar situation comes up, they already know how to handle it because they have experience in addressing a difficult situation. That is my parenting philosophy: maximum efficiency means maximum impact using minimum energy. That is the magic formula that works for me.

Taking away hard things for my kids is also not something that I do. I learned early on that no matter how diligent I am or how hard I try, it is impossible to prevent hard things from happening to my kids. Learning this though was something that entirely changed my perspective. That is the point when I began to realize that my number one goal was to teach them how to handle their own problems rather than taking away their problems.

A few years ago, when Ella was only eight, I took the kids on a backpacking trip with some other families. We decided to hike into Fossil Springs and camp for a few days. It is beautiful there with turquoise waters and caves to swim in. The only way to get there is by hiking in. It's about four miles off the closest road through some steep terrain. I talked to the kids ahead of time about how hard the hike would be and whether or not they thought they could do it. We would be carrying twenty-five pound packs with all the gear and food necessary for camping for a few days. They all decided they wanted to do it and since I'm always up for an adventure, we made our plans. We got to the hiking trail early and got everyone's packs put on. The packs were taller than our heads and very heavy. The first few miles of the hike went fairly well. Then it got hot. And steep. And we got tired. Some of the other younger kids in the group had given their packs to their parents to carry. The parents had the extra packs on the front of their bodies then their own packs on the back. I don't even know how they could walk! Ella told me she was tired and asked if I would carry her pack. I said "Sorry Sweet Pea but you've got to carry your own pack."

She walked a little longer and then asked me again. I declined and said that we'd talked about how hard this was going to be and everyone had agreed to carry their own packs. I told her I knew how hard this was and that if any little girlie could do this, it was her. She did not like my answer. She cried and told me that the other moms were carrying packs for their kids.

I felt like a bit of a heel but still told her that I was sorry, I wouldn't be carrying her pack but asked her if she'd like a back massage. She was pretty steamed but who can turn down a back massage? We stopped and took our packs off for a few minutes while I massaged her back. Then I put my own pack back on and asked her if she'd like to hike with me or without me. She was still a little mad so she said she wanted to hike without me. I told her "Good luck Girlie!" then turned and started back on the trail. I went around the corner and couldn't see her anymore. I knew there were still people behind us and she wouldn't get left but I also knew no one else would carry her pack and hoped that she would be ok. When we got to our camping spot a few hours later, she came running over to me so excited that she had done it! She had done a really hard thing by carrying her own pack on this steep hike. I gave her a big hug and congratulated her on a job well done. She told me that when we hiked out, her goal was to be up in the front with the bigger kids and to hike without complaining. She made me smile and I remembered why I don't take away hard things from my kids even if I can.

Are you still feeling unnecessary guilt about your parenting? Do you think this might not work with your family? Are you feeling like you can't turn this type of responsibility over to your kids because they're probably going to blow it? Guess what? My family isn't perfect either. Sometimes we blow it too. I have fantastic kids but they occasionally make poor choices without thinking through the consequences. This doesn't mean I'm a bad mom. This doesn't even mean my kids are bad kids. All this means is we're all still in the process of learning. The great news is we will be in this process of learning for our entire lives! At no point ever will we have arrived at the point where we don't make poor choices anymore. That means we will be making mistakes as long as we're living. Guess what else? That's part of the plan. Heavenly Father is perfectly ok with us making mistakes and making poor choices. We have his permission to make poor choices and learn from them. I think that's the most important thing he looks at. He cares what choices we make but he cares more about what we learn from those choices. He cares if we grow as a person from that choice and when the situation comes up again, are we able to make a better choice? This is true for us and it's also true for our kids. I am not on trial of whether or not I'm a great parent depending on what type of choices my kids are making. My job as a parent is to teach, which I do. My job as a parent is not to prevent any bad thing from happening to them or prevent them from ever making mistakes or bad choices. Having this attitude takes so much pressure and guilt out of the parenting equation and since I am anti-pressure and anti-guilt, having this frame of mind works for me.

Last summer one of my sons was running around the neighborhood with his friends pool hopping. When you live in Arizona in the summer time, that is about the only thing you can do outside when it's one hundred and fifteen degrees. He went to one of his friends' homes and they all got the great idea of jumping off her two story house into the pool. Noooot a great idea. After finding out about this, I talked to the friends' mom and let her know that I had spoken with him and he would not be jumping off her roof anymore. She said she had been worried and wasn't sure if I knew. I apologized for his worrying her then told her to feel free to share information about my kids that she thought I needed to know and that I couldn't guarantee they wouldn't make bad choices but I could guarantee I would address it when it happened. As a parent, that's all I can do. Teach and consequence. I cannot prevent my kids from making bad choices. Having this mindset prevents so much guilt. Guilt is an energy-sucker and a wasted emotion. Nothing good comes from feeling guilty over things you did or didn't do perfectly.

When Sam was little, he went through a hitting phase. Every kid I know has gone through this phase. As a parent, it's no fun. One day Ella and Sam were playing while my mom was up visiting me. Some conflict arose between them (happens with three and four year olds) which ensued in a little fisty-cuff. Sam had resorted to hitting. After sending him to his room to cool-off, I told my mom that this was not a fun stage. She said "You just need to teach your kids not to hit." Hmmm. So I responded with "I actually teach my kids to hit. I tell them violence solves everything." We started laughing because of course I'm teaching my kids not to hit! But just because I teach it doesn't mean they're always going to do it. My job is to consequence and give them the tools to make a different choice next time which I do. In Sam's case, it was role playing how to use his words. I use that phrase a lot with my kids. "Use your words." And "Respect others' words." This basic lesson on communication solves a lot of our family conflicts and it's a good reminder for me as well to not act out my frustrations, but instead to let the kids know with my words why I am upset or unhappy about something. It also lets them know they need to listen to people in the family and see the situation from someone else's point of view.

I was talking to Sam a little while ago over some situation that had happened that I wasn't happy with. After discussing the situation, Sam said to me "I like how you let us explain our side of the story. I like how you let us talk instead of just yell at us." The reason I do this is because understanding the motivation behind the behavior is almost more important to me than the behavior itself. Let me explain. But first you need to know something more about me. I love power tools. My very favorite birthday gift ever was a Ryobi power drill set that came with one hundred different bits. There is even a bit that drills through concrete! It makes my heart race every time I put my hands on the case. I am very handy around the house and can fix nearly anything. One of my friends nicknamed me "Barb the Builder." I love to take on home repair projects and that is an understatement.

One afternoon when my kids were very little, I decided they needed a secret room to play in and I had the perfect place. Our closet under the stairs didn't go back very far and there was a lot of inaccessible space. I decided I would saw through the drywall and turn that into their secret room. Well, that was a long time ago before I realized how much I loved tools and since my husband was not handy, I didn't have anything that would work to cut through the drywall. That didn't stop me. I was determined to make a secret room that day. So I took a large butcher knife from the kitchen and started hacking away. Just for your information, butcher knives do not work very well as saws and then after using them as saws, they also do not work very well as butcher knives. I quickly realized I I needed something more so I made a trip to the nearest Home Depot and bought tools and supplies that I thought I would need. I framed the doorway out, dry-walled inside the room since it was just studs and finished with some carpet. It was awesome and the kids loved it. They spent hours in there every day which gave me my cleaning time. Adam was very surprised when he came home from work that day.

I've done all sorts of things like that. I've built and decorated a beautiful playhouse for Ella complete with a pink kitchen set and wired with tiny pink lights. I've made a five foot, four tiered chandelier for my two story living room which turned out amazing. I don't ever have plans for these things, I just think them up in my head and start tinkering. My point is I've always got tools out. One afternoon when Sam was four I came downstairs and saw three huge holes in the wall. There was a screwdriver sticking out of one of the holes and nails and screws all over the wall. It didn't take me long to realize Sam was the culprit. I was very unhappy as I like my house to be undamaged but took the time to talk to him and ask why he did that. It turns out he just wanted to use my tools. He wanted to build something too. I went back to Home Depot and bought him his own tool box along with huge blocks of wood that he could hammer, drill and saw to his heart's content. He actually didn't even get in trouble for what he did (though he did have to help me repair it). The reason is he wasn't trying to be destructive. He just wanted to build a project. Understanding their motivations behind the behavior helps me know what I need to address as a parent. Was it a bad attitude? Were they trying to rebel? Did they not think all the way through the consequences of that choice? Understanding where they're coming from helps me to come up with an appropriate consequence for them to learn.

Above all, my primary focus as a parent is to build relationships with my kids and to teach them. Building relationships doesn't necessarily take a lot of energy the same way that cooking, cleaning and running a house by myself does. All it takes is focus on the right things. I am very happy with my family life at home. I have terrific kids and I have great relationships with all of them. Sam who is fourteen, gives me hugs every time I walk by him. We probably hug ten times a day. Every time he hugs me I tell him "You're such a great kid." He always responds with "You're such a great mom." He makes my heart melt.

There are some days I handle things with my kids and I think "Man, I handled that just right." But there are also days when I handle things and I think "Man, that was a train wreck." I just reset and try again the next day. My kids aren't perfect kids and I am not a perfect mom, but we are happy. I parent exactly the way I want to and very on purpose. Having mental illness has forced me to really dig down deep and figure out precisely what the most important things are for me to do. And those are all I do. That's it. I only do the most important things. My most important things may not be the same as your most important things. You get to decide what your priorities are with your own family. Once you've ferreted them out though, spend your time doing your own most important things. Make sure you are parenting on purpose and not wasting energy in places that aren't on the top of your list. That is how you can make parenting enjoyable and successful even if you have a mental illness and you too will be a super awesome mom.

CHAPTER 9

KEEPIN' IT TOGETHER

(Marriage and other Family Relationships)

● ● ●

MARRIAGE IS A TRICKY TOPIC and one I am hesitant to talk about because it's so personal. However my editor friend convinced me this chapter needs to be in here. I definitely would have appreciated the help with how to make our marriage work and what it would mean for us when I was first diagnosed. Even though this is written with marriage in mind, the same relationship principles apply to anyone with a loved one struggling with mental illness whether that's a parent, child, family member or friend. I'm a little bit apprehensive about this but I will give it my best shot. Even though I've been married for eighteen years and have a great relationship with my husband, I don't feel like I can spout marital wisdom because I am only half of the equation. I only know things from my perspective. I thought the only way to get a good picture of how to make a relationship with mental illness work is to rope in my better half, Adam. He has amazing insights and has helped me tremendously as we've learned together how to navigate this weighty issue. We're going to have what my son Max calls "Real Talk." This is where all the walls are down and there is some very open, very real communication. Real Talk means no judgment, anything can be said and it has to be kept confidential. Those are the rules. So here we go with some Real Talk.

So Adam, thank you for agreeing to participate.

I'm getting paid for this, right?

Absolutely. You can have full access to all the money in our joint checking account. Also I just want you to know that there are no wrong answers but if you say things that make me look good I'll bake you a chocolate molten lava cake with fresh raspberries.

Deal.

So before we jump in, I want people to have a picture of where we started. I think understanding our relationship initially and then how the mental illness diagnosis affected us and how we dealt with it will help people who are going through it.

Agreed.

So what attracted you to me in the first place?

Initially your hot body. Just kidding, don't say that. Although I'm really not kidding.

Too late this is Real Talk. That means no editing. Plus you're really looking good now for that chocolate cake.

Ok one of the things that I was attracted to was that you were such a hard worker. You set goals and accomplished so many things. You were very athletic and intelligent. You had a testimony of the Gospel and served a mission and you gave it your all. You just worked hard. You even put off marrying me to go on a mission. You had a heightened level of dedication and commitment. As hard as it was to watch you leave to serve a mission, I did like it or at least was impressed by it because you set a goal and were committed to it so you did it.

What was our relationship like when we were first married?

I think it was like two capable people partnering up with each other but doing their own thing. For example, you had a scholarship to go to BYU but then I got a scholarship to go to law school so we separated for a few semesters so we could both accomplish our schooling goals. Not a relationship separation, we were just working on our own things together. We were in love but it was sort of like we'll just both accomplish our individual goals under the same roof. We were probably more focused on our individual goals rather than building our marriage. When we were first married I didn't think marriage required a ton of work. I thought if you married the right person and you liked each other then Boom! You automatically had a great marriage. That's what I thought.

You don't think so now?

Uh, no. (Laughing) Good marriages don't just happen naturally. They take a lot of work and a lot of focused effort. I realized I can't pursue my own goals at the expense of the marriage. I underestimated the amount of time it would take to build our relationship and I underestimated the drain on the relationship when I was not actively doing things to make it better. In other words, it was a lack of making deposits in the relationship bank. I didn't even know what deposits were or what was important and meaningful to you. I didn't know what you needed.

I was pretty self-sufficient. I didn't ask for a lot from you because I thought I could do it myself. I could handle it.

You could and you were fine. That's one of the things I liked about you. You were very confident in who you were and what you wanted so I figured you could do your thing and I could do mine and we would regroup periodically and live under the same roof.

And kiss whenever we want.

Right. And kiss whenever we want.

I always thought our marriage was good though.

So did I. We had fun. We enjoyed being around each other. That didn't require work because I've always enjoyed being around you. But a good marriage requires more than just being around somebody and having fun. Because if you don't do certain things (like make emotional deposits) then it gets to a point when your spouse is not happy.

I thought the same thing. I didn't realize how high of a priority we would have to put on the relationship. We would have to sacrifice other things for it to be successful. You really can't have it all as far as professional goals, individual goals and still have personal success in relationships and with your family.

In the beginning I thought it was a strength that we pursued our individual goals and that we didn't need each other that much. I felt like in the beginning we didn't need each other but we chose each other. Now I feel like we need each other. It's not like you're just a great girl I like to hang out with. I think it's a fallacy that your marriage is stronger if you're both so independent that you can actually do your own thing-- like a power couple.

I felt like we were a power couple when we first got married.

Yes, we were both very capable, ambitious and energetic. We had both served missions and had lofty schooling goals. We were ready to attack the world.

So when some of the symptoms of mental illness started to become more severe, when everything was falling apart and I was not able to do the things that I normally did, what did you think? Did you think I was just lazy?

No. I never thought you were lazy. I knew you too well for that. You were pregnant at the time and we had little kids and I just thought it must be really hard to be pregnant. It must be really hard to be home taking care of kids all day and I just didn't know because I was at work. I've never been pregnant and I didn't know how you felt or what it did to your body or energy levels. I just tried to be understanding and figured you were doing the best you could.

You were very understanding. It made me love you more and realize that I could count on you to support me with anything. Having you be so non-judgemental was a huge factor in me talking to you as openly and honestly as I did which ultimately led to me getting the support I needed. I was so critical of myself and frustrated that I couldn't do the things I felt like I should be able to do. If you had been critical in any way, that would have confirmed what I already thought about myself. I wouldn't have seen the good in myself. I would have discounted all my efforts because the results were so miniscule. I felt like I couldn't do anything! You have been my biggest cheerleader and have helped me to have a better perspective on myself and my efforts and the world around me. You are my anchor. Plus you make me laugh.

So when all of this was going down, what did you initially do?

I had to spend time to understand it. I really had no idea what bipolar was. I didn't know anything about mental illness. I had to search and get educated so I could understand you better and how our marriage could be good.

How did you do that?

Mostly by listening to you. You spent a lot of time reading everything you could get a hold of and trying to learn and understand what mental illness was. You were constantly reading everything and then you would tell me what you read. I also learned by watching and really trying to understand things from your perspective. I had to get outside myself, which is something all good husbands need to do, but I had more of an urgency to do that. I couldn't afford to just float along in my marriage. I didn't have that option. This was a crisis. This was urgent. I had to make a focused effort to learn and understand your mindset and your perspective on things and I had to make some adjustments. I think we have communicated more because of it. We've had more deep, soul searching and heartfelt conversations because of it than we would have if you were Miss Go-Getter doing a million things and we were just floating along together in life. I truly believe that the struggle with mental illness has made our marriage better. Because of these challenges we were forced to open up and dig deep and communicate thoughts and feelings. We were forced to do this. It is not something that came easily for me. It was certainly outside my comfort zone. But now that we've done it I look back and think that is absolutely the best thing we could have done to strengthen our marriage.

Initially did you feel like this was the end of our happiness or life as we knew it?

Yes, initially that thought did cross my mind. I just didn't understand it at all. I had nobody to talk to about it. I felt entirely ill-equipped.

I wasn't a psychologist or psychiatrist. I thought I don't know how to do this. You talk about your goal for a while was just don't die, but honestly for a while there my goal was just stay together. Just get one more day. Not that divorce was an option but I just didn't know if you were going to make it. I was concerned that if I didn't do it correctly or if I mishandled it, I would lose you and it seemed like a lot of pressure for someone who had no training to figure out. I just felt like I don't know how I'm supposed to do this. I don't know how I'm supposed to help you. That's when I just started focusing on what I loved about you, instead of the little day-to-day things that really weren't that important. That's when the house was messy and you were struggling just to get off the couch. I began thinking I'm just happy you're here and we're married. Regarding the other stuff maybe we'll get to a point where we can do it but maybe not. My goal was to just keep us together. I didn't know how to do that so I just took it one day at a time and hoped and prayed I'd figure it out.

What helped you to do that?

One thing that helped was going with you to psychiatrists and doctors appointments. That helped me understand you much better. I began seeing the world through your perspective. It's hard to understand unless you're there listening to the doctor and listening to your spouse. I began to understand things better when I was part of the conversation with your doctors.

That was helpful for me when you came to appointments. I felt a lot of moral support when you would take time off work to be with me helping me understand and work through this hard thing. Missing work spoke a lot to me since even when each of the kids were born, you never missed more than a day of work. I would still be in the hospital with a new baby and you were already back at the office. You really never missed work before for anything so the fact that you would voluntarily come during the day to my appointments just to support me meant a lot.

Yes, I learned that going to doctor's appointments was very helpful to both of us. I certainly didn't go to every doctor appointment that you had but I could tell in talking to you which ones were important for me to go to and which ones were more routine. There were also times when the doctor wanted to meet with you alone, but those were rare. Going to the doctor appointments with you not only helped me learn about mental illness from a professional perspective but it also helped me better understand how you felt and to see things from your perspective. I could also hear what the psychiatrist or psychologist was saying to you and I could then reinforce that.

Sometimes, in the past, I've felt like I wasn't pulling my weight in the marriage even though you didn't say that. When I was really down, I felt like I wasn't contributing anything. During those times what did I do for you?

You did a lot of things for me. Surprisingly, one of the biggest things you did for me was to be happy when I got home from work. You would smile, give me a hug and a kiss and we would just sit on the couch and watch a movie together. That was a huge help to me. That was a big deal. Maybe the house wasn't perfectly clean and maybe we were having cold cereal for dinner but having you smile and connect with me, even when you weren't feeling great meant a lot. These small and simple things held our marriage together when times were tough.

Did you ever feel like you were carrying too much of the weight?

No. You were carrying much more of the weight than I ever did with mental illness. I could see the weight you were carrying and all the effort you were exerting every day to lift the heavy burden. It takes an enormous amount of strength and toughness to fight mental illness. It is important to understand and appreciate the tremendous effort it takes for your spouse to push forward each day.

I felt like I was being crushed by this weight. I was barely surviving but I felt like from the outside no one could possibly know how hard it was just to make it through a day. How did you see the level of effort it took for me?

I could see just by watching you and living with you. I knew what a hard worker you were and I knew if there was any way possible for you to be doing these other things, you would be doing them. I learned by talking to you and over time I started understanding more. I understood by going to doctor appointments and reading books. But honestly during the difficult times I prayed a lot, to better understand your struggles and to know how I could help. Over time I began to see you as an elite spiritual athlete going through difficult training.

I think that's something you've been good at from the beginning is appreciating the heavy weight that this has been. I think that's not always the case in marriages with mental illness. You were always very encouraging to me when I was struggling and that was helpful in so many ways. You did a lot of things that made the weight easier. What do you think the biggest thing is to tell the spouse?

Be part of the solution. If you're not part of the solution then you're part of the problem. Look for the good in your spouse. Praise them. Don't underestimate the power of a genuine compliment. It is hard because you can't take this challenge away from them. You're very limited to what you can do to help. But what you can do you should do. Just don't add to the burden through insensitive actions and comments.

Some spouses get very frustrated when they don't see things getting done. They feel like there's not enough effort and can be very hard on the person dealing with mental illness.

I think that's how some spouses deal with it partly because they don't understand it. They themselves are struggling to understand what's going on and why life is different. The most important thing you can do is to focus on the positive. It is also important to be patient and realize that improvement will take time. It can take weeks or months but probably not years. Be willing to lift when necessary. It could seem like an eternity but it really won't be that long if the person struggling is taking the necessary steps to stabilize. Just realize that there's going to be a time, a relatively short period of time, that things will be challenging but don't give up. You just have to put one foot in front of the other. Keep holding it together. Focus on the positive and lift your spouse's burden.

Going through that stage though felt like an eternity to me. I didn't know if I would make it through. I wish I had someone telling me it wouldn't last forever. I wish I had known how long it would take to stabilize. I think that would have taken away some of the panic that I felt.

Yes, the scariest time was when you were in crisis, the time between diagnosis and the time you finally stabilized. This is a critical time. Spouses need to know what to do in crisis. If you have a plan of action it is less scary.

Finding the right medication though does take time and it's a distressing and scary time because you don't know when it will end.

Unfortunately there are no short cuts, no quick fixes. Long term stability takes time. I think one of the most important exercises during this time period is to focus on what you love about your spouse and why you married them, even when the house is a mess and even when they haven't showered. Can you find something positive?

Can you make a genuine compliment? The answer is yes. You can. You can always find a genuine compliment if that's your mindset.

That's something that you did for me during a very difficult time. Every morning when I woke up there would be a post-it note on the bathroom counter with something you loved about me. There was a huge variety of things that you wrote and you got very creative. That meant a lot to me because at that point it was difficult to even get out of bed. Knowing that there was a note there, wondering what it would say, that got me out of bed on those mornings.

That had the double benefit of requiring me to focus on your strengths and what I love about you while articulating the things you needed to hear from me to give you encouragement and strength to keep pushing and fighting as well. It can be very easy to lose perspective. It can happen in all marriages but it can be more difficult where mental illness is a factor because it's such an all-consuming issue. You can easily lose perspective. When that happens, your marriage can fall apart. Just staying anchored on why you love your spouse, why you married them, what their strengths are, those are the things that will keep your marriage together. That's what will help you make it.

I felt like I wasn't me for a while, like I was living in a parallel universe. It was very surreal. I didn't know how to get back.

The true "you" was always there, it's just that the weight of mental illness was pushing you down. I always knew that as soon as we figured out how to lift the enormous burden then the true "you" would be able to shine through again. I think it helps when somebody reminds you of who you are. I think we could have shortened the crisis period if I had done the post-It note exercise sooner.

Did you ever feel like I wasn't myself?

Yes, when you're in the depths of despair – in crisis mode. There were times when it was scary because it wasn't you. It's not like it went on for a long time but when you were at the bottom, when you were suicidal, talking to you, looking at you, interacting with you, it was scary because it wasn't you. It ties back to stabilization. The medication wasn't working. Medication is a vital part of stabilization. The right medication lifted the burden and weight of mental illness enough so that your personality could shine through again. Stabilization is the key to success.

That was a difficult time period but your post-it notes helped me get through it. I still have all those post-its taped to the closet door. When I'm feeling down, I go in and read them. I think this is a hard area for the spouse though. Talking with other friends who struggle or have spouses who struggle with mental illness, a lot of them don't see anything good or have anything good to say to the one struggling. Any thoughts on that?

I think sometimes spouses feel like they're enabling by complimenting or somehow indicating that they are satisfied with how things currently are. They feel like how can I condone this? I don't want to condone this cycle or they'll just keep doing this. This is how it will be for the rest of the marriage. They're afraid to give compliments during crisis time because they're afraid it will send the wrong message that this is how I like things. I think some spouses feel almost like they need to train the one struggling and push them out of this struggle they're in. The fact is the person comes out of this on their own. Just don't be an impediment. Your job is to clear the way. Make it as easy as possible and help lift the burden.

That's what you realized as time went on and when you did, you started helping me lift the burden. You were never critical but eventually you started learning what was helpful. It meant a lot to me that you were very generous with your compliments and encouragement. Having you verbalize those things and tell me what a champion I was made me view myself differently. It changed my perspective more than having other people telling me that. I think that's because you lived with me. You saw the worst of it. You saw all the ugly and if, after seeing all of that, you still had good things to say, then it must be true. How did you know that would work?

I didn't know what would help. I just figured that being positive and seeing the good in you couldn't hurt. The proof of what works is how it made you feel. If it lifted the burden then it worked. The right answer is do whatever your spouse needs for them to feel more support and more love. Those were just ideas that I had to make it through and build a better relationship.

Was there ever a point where you thought this is way too much work? Or it's never going to get better?

I knew it was going to require a little bit of change on my part but I underestimated how much change. The turning point for me was the suicide attempt. I was still trying to pursue my own goals. I was spending a lot of time in my church calling and was still very ambitious at work. I knew you needed help but I underestimated what you needed from me. The suicide attempt is when it really hit me. I realized I didn't need to tweak how I was and what my priorities were, I needed an overhaul. I needed to change dramatically to have any meaningful impact. A little turn here and there was not enough. I had to make a major course correction if we were going to be successful.

Like what?

Like my time commitment to being with you and communicating with you because we didn't communicate all that much. I'd go to work and come home. We would then deal with the kids and homework and running the family. We might have a few minutes to talk and catch up then we'd go to bed. Every so often I would call during the day to check in. I then realized how important that was to you but to me it seemed unnecessary because I had work to do. That seemed to be a lot of talking. I thought I didn't have time to talk during the day. That wasn't true but that was just my mindset. My mindset was when I'm at work I will work and then we can talk when I get home. I know there was a little bit of tension over that and you sometimes felt like I wasn't there for you.

I didn't ask for much in our relationship because I could usually do it myself. It was really hard to ask you to call me during the day. When I finally did ask you and you didn't do it, that was a big hit for me.

I didn't realize how important that was. I just thought you were saying we should try to do this. If you would have said on a scale from one to ten this is a ten, I would have done it but I didn't know. This was one of those small course corrections that I had to make.

That's something that has definitely changed once you knew how important it was to me. You call me a lot now. You have a long commute to work and we talk all the way in, you call me at lunch, then we often talk on the way home as well.

Yes, we frequently talk two or three times a day and not just "Hi, how are you?" or a quick text but very long, deep conversations about everything.

I think that's when I started to feel like I had help. Before that I still felt like I was in it on my own a lot of the time.

That's probably what led to the suicide attempt, me not making enough adjustments fast enough and big enough. I wasn't communicating that I'm on board with you. I'm here to help and it's not just you on your own. My conduct was saying you have to deal with this on your own but I didn't know that's what I was communicating. I thought I was just being ambitious and setting goals and accomplishing things and doing good things. I thought that's what I was supposed to be doing as a husband.

Was the suicide attempt what changed everything? Did it change overnight?

Yes on both of those. That shook me to my core and I realized I'm just a moment away from not having you. I had no idea that I was that close to losing you. I thought I was making adjustments but it wasn't enough. It wasn't soon enough. That's when I realized this is bigger than setting goals at work or my church calling or anything else I'm doing. There's nothing more important than figuring this out together. Ideally we could have communicated with each other to accomplish the same thing before that happened but I don't think we were great communicators.

I also don't think that I realized I was there either. I knew I was doing poorly but I had been struggling for a while. I knew I thought about suicide a lot but I thought I was strong enough, that I was thinking clearly enough and could handle it. I didn't realize how much I needed you.

That was a tough time period trying to juggle work and family because the way I was juggling it previously wasn't working but I didn't know how to do it any other way. It was hard. Some mornings I could tell you weren't doing well but I had to go to work. I couldn't lose my job so I would call and check in but there was a lot of anxiety while I was at work wondering how you were doing at home. That was complicated by the fact that you didn't have anybody at the time that you were willing and able to talk to other than me. I think that's something people need to realize that it doesn't replace the spouse but it is helpful if you have one or two other people you can talk to.

I didn't want anyone to know. I had family that was willing to talk and friends I could have approached but I didn't want anyone to know how bad it really was. I didn't think they could help so I wondered what's the point? Why drag everyone down and let them see what a mess things are if there's ultimately nothing they can do which isn't true by the way. Having someone listen and be supportive, having them check in on you to ask how you are helps a lot.

It really is a downward spiral. You don't want people to know so you can't be around them because if you are, they'll know. Then you isolate yourself which leaves you alone with your confused thinking which is not good. That was a really challenging stretch.

That's when I needed a counselor. I was willing to talk but definitely not willing to discuss with family and friends. That's when you made major corrections as you call them.

Yes, I made major corrections. I made adjustments in church service. My calling didn't change but I changed how I did it. I knew I had to do things differently. I could still accept callings but I knew I had to do them differently. I knew that you had to come first. I thought

I put your needs ahead of church service but I think sometimes I fell short. I learned that there is a possibility of serving too much in the church. You have to be sensitive to the needs of your family and cut back if necessary. I talked to our bishop at the time and he was entirely supportive of that. Basically I started cutting back on everything that I was doing. I used other people to do the work instead of me doing it all myself which is kind of how I did things before. Anything that needed to be done, even if it was small and easily delegated, I would do it myself. That's what changed. I started prioritizing and delegating to other people because I couldn't do it alone.

I don't remember our circumstances changing much. I was released but you still had your calling. You still went to work but your availability to me was drastically different.

When you called me or I needed to call you, I tried to make that a higher priority than my work or my clients which was not the case before. Before I felt like work time was work time and I couldn't really do much else.

I think I started understanding what things I needed help with and began to ask for them and to explain what was important. There was a lot more communication between us.

Yes, our communication changed drastically.

Do you think it's unfair to be married to someone with mental illness? Did you draw the short straw?

Absolutely not. On the contrary, I think working through mental illness together has made our marriage so much better than it would have been otherwise. For a marriage to be successful each side has to be willing to give 100%. This is true in any marriage. Mental illness is just one thing a couple could struggle with. I guess the whole point is it doesn't matter what the challenges are in marriage, you're either going to work together to overcome them or you're not. You are an amazing person. Mental illness didn't change that.

There were times you would tell me I was an amazing person but it was hard to believe that was true sometimes because having mental illness made me feel like I was inherently flawed. Did you ever feel like you were beating your head against a brick wall because I didn't believe what you were telling me?

Yes there have been times where I would tell you what I was thinking and feeling and you wouldn't believe it. It was very frustrating and I felt like there was nothing more I could do. I wished that somehow you would be able to see the situation more clearly. Becoming stable on the medications helped you to do that.

It took a long time to find the right medication. Did you ever wonder if it would work?

I always believed you would stabilize, I just didn't know how happy we were capable of being in light of the mental illness. I sometimes thought during the process, have we peaked? Is this the maximum level of happiness (which wasn't tremendous) that we would ever achieve? It was very difficult to think about you being that unhappy for the rest of your life.

I feel like you became more helpful in stages but I also feel like I got better in stages. Starting on the right medication was big boost to help me function normally but after that even when I switched medications, it was still hard but there wasn't the same sort of panic because I knew I could be stable. It just takes time.

It's just hard to be patient with the process. Too many times we're impatient and want change from day to day or week to week. The change is not going to happen that fast. It won't take years but it's also not going to be better in a day or even a week. It's going to take some time. Just be patient and let it naturally happen. You can't force it to happen faster. It's an organic thing that builds. Stability is not a quick fix. It's a slow and steady process but that's how a stable foundation is built. It's slow and steady improvement.

It's true that this has definitely helped me become more patient with the process, myself and other people. It also helped me realize what things were important to me.

That's one thing that I've felt like mental illness has changed in you. You have a deep level of compassion and patience and understanding for other people and their trials. Before it seemed like you were box-checking. It was trophies and awards and outward recognition for accomplishment. I feel like the struggle with mental illness has made you excel as a person, as a human being where there are no awards

*and acknowledgements and prizes or rankings but you've become a
better person.*

It's been helpful to me that you recognize this and point it out
to me because a lot of time s along the way I just felt like I
was digressing in every area. Having you see the areas I was
growing in and pointing them out has helped me change my
perspective. It helped me realize that I could be a better person
because of this and I think I am. This is sort of like when we
were first married and I felt like I was such a patient person.
After we had kids I felt like I digressed. I felt like I had less
patience. You were kind enough to point out that I definitely
had more patience after kids than before. It's just that I wasn't
as aware of my flaws (laughing).

You're welcome.

So are there other things I've done to make it easier?

*You are more in tune with how you're feeling and you make adjust-
ments in your life so you don't get to a crisis. The fewer crises we have
the better. You read a lot of books on marriage, parenting, mental
illness, really anything that you think would help you. You definitely
made our relationship a priority. So my question for you: Has that
changed over time?*

Absolutely. My number one focus now is on all my relationships and that's it. My relationship with Heavenly Father, my

relationship with you, with the kids, that's always my top priority and it definitely wasn't in the past.

Over time there's been an evolution for both of us and a change from accomplishing things to developing personally and developing relationships with others. You don't get awards for any of that stuff and so a lot of times in life we neglect our relationships.

I realized that none of that mattered. When I was in the hospital after the suicide attempt I realized that no awards mattered. The only things I was thinking about were the kids and you.

I think we both went through a wake-up call. For me the suicide attempt made me realize how important our relationship was and that I could actually lose you. Sometimes you take people for granted and something wakes you up to say Wow! I never thought that this could happen. I realized I didn't want that to happen and it made me step it up more. I realized this is life or death. I had to ask myself how much do I value our marriage? At that point I realized work doesn't matter. I had to work so we had money but really none of it mattered. I had to ask myself is it worth fighting for? Every marriage has to answer that question at some point. When mental illness is part of the marriage it is no different.

What are things I do that make it harder?

I would say discounting compliments and not believing me when I tell you things.

It's hard. I still struggle in my head with believing them. I've really had to work on accepting compliments.

It was hard trying to help you see that you were important to me and you were important to the family. I felt like I did everything in my power to articulate, explain and persuade you how important and necessary you were to our family and to our marriage and you just didn't believe me. You genuinely thought we'd be better off without you. That was the most frustrating belief that you had in your head and I couldn't effectively persuade you otherwise.

It's true. Is there anything else that makes it harder?

When you overcommit and overextend to the point where you're burned out, that makes it harder.

Always when I overcommit it's to things outside our marriage and family. That's what everybody else sees. It's still sometimes hard to look bad to other people, like I'm not willing to help or I'm not willing to serve when really I'm just trying to make sure that my limited energy is being allocated to my top priority which is my family. The family is who suffers when I burn out and now I'm not willing to let the family suffer which means everywhere else it can look like I won't help or I'm not dedicated.

Yes but that's not really true. It just means that you're being responsible with your energy budget.

Sometimes it was hard for me to go to church. Did you ever worry about that?

No. I never felt like you came home early or didn't want to go to church because you didn't have a testimony. I knew it was just socially difficult for you to be there and interact with people because you were on the verge of crying and you didn't want to talk to anyone.

It had nothing to do with any struggle of faith, it was more of a social challenge. It's not just that I didn't want to be around people, which was true, but sometimes the message that came across to me at church just made me feel worse. During lessons or talking with people they would say if you're struggling read your scriptures and say your prayers. First, I felt like they just don't get it. They don't understand. Doing those things is not enough to lift my heavy burden. Secondly, a part of me (a very small part) thought maybe they're right and if I just tried harder or was a better person then maybe I wouldn't be struggling with this.

I know you may have felt like that but it wasn't true. Some people don't understand because they don't have experience with it. They just need to become more educated. Secondly though, struggling with mental illness has nothing to do with you not trying hard enough or being a better person. You are one of the best people I know.

What do you wish you had known in the beginning?

Everything in this book.

So true.

Really though, this would have been so helpful. It would have been helpful because it would have given me a greater understanding of how to address things before they turned into a crisis. I wish I would have known earlier that when you say you're "done," you're done. That means right now. Immediately. This second. I was more casual about it before. I thought yeah, we can work on that as soon as we're done with this or maybe at the end of the week when things aren't so busy but that's not the case with you. When you hit your limit, we need to start cancelling things or making other arrangements immediately.

That's something that took me a little while to learn too. Now, no matter what I'm doing, if I feel like I'm done, I stop immediately. If I'm in the middle of cooking dinner I turn it over to the kids and go to my room. If I'm out running errands I leave immediately and come home without finishing my errands. If we've got a busy week I start cutting things out so I can have quiet time at home. That's something that helps me avoid the crisis situation.

Yes, that's something that we've both learned.

If you could share one piece of advice to a spouse of someone newly diagnosed, what would it be?

I would say stay focused on what you love about your spouse. Hold on to that while you work through the issues and be patient with the process. I think it's important because the challenges can overwhelm you. You can get hyper-focused on what seems to be going wrong. When all you do is see the negative things or the challenges you can lose sight of the beautiful person you chose to marry and the importance of what you're fighting for.

Are you happy? Do you feel like our life is better now than it would have been without mental illness?

Yes, absolutely to both. Our marriage is better than I had ever imagined that it could be. I feel like there's been sort of a renaissance after the struggle in the last few years. There's just happiness and excitement and good communication. I don't know how to express it right. It's like marriage starts out great and exciting then life happens and kids happen and struggles happen and I feel like we just kind of caught a second wind. I feel energized and happy and look forward to coming home every night. I would rather spend time with you than anyone else.

You definitely get the chocolate cake. Any last thoughts?

Yes. When do I get my cake?

There it is people, Real Talk. Good stuff right? Now remember the last rule: this has to be kept confidential. That means this stays between you and me and the other thousands of people who read this book.

CHAPTER 10

Life is a Gym

• • •

C.S. LEWIS HAD A WONDERFUL analogy about God working with us to help us improve and grow as individuals. "Imagine yourself as a living house. God comes in to rebuild that house. At first, perhaps, you can understand what He is doing. He is getting the drains right and stopping the leaks in the roof and so on; you knew that those jobs needed doing and so you are not surprised. But presently He starts knocking the house about in a way that hurts abominably and does not seem to make any sense. What on earth is He up to? The explanation is that He is building quite a different house from the one you thought of - throwing out a new wing here, putting on an extra floor there, running up towers, making courtyards. You thought you were being made into a decent little cottage: but He is building a palace. He intends to come and live in it Himself."

I love that analogy. Heavenly Father's goal is to work with us to become the best person we can possibly be. Sometimes it's painful. Sometimes we don't feel like it's going well. But always if we trust in Him we'll have better results than if we were to do it on our own.

I have a different analogy. I think life is like a gym and Heavenly Father is our personal trainer. Imagine going in to your local fitness club and meeting with a trainer. Imagine that instead of meeting with you to discuss your personal fitness needs and goals, he simply handed you a sheet with the following:

Workout: 50 pushups
                            3 x 10 100 lb squats
                            3 mile run

Maybe this trainer has years of experience and has found that this workout is the average of what he has recommended to clients over the years. This may or may not work for you. If you're new to the gym ain't no way fifty pushups are ever going to happen (even if they're the sissy knee push-ups). Five might be a better goal for someone new. What if you're coming back from an injury and your goal is to strengthen the areas that have been weakened? If you want to strengthen your core and back muscles then this workout is no good and the squats could actually injure you further. What if you're training for a race or event and cardio is the main thing you need? If the bulk of your workout is spent on weights, you won't be ready. The point is it doesn't matter if this workout would best fit an average person because you are not average. You are unique and special and your needs will be very individually tailored to you because of that. If this trainer doesn't take the time to sit and talk with you and thoroughly understand what your goals are, what your current situation is and what your background has been, there is no way he can come up with a plan that will optimize the time you spend in the gym and give you the best results. He needs to know if your goal is to lose weight. He needs to know if your goal is to lower your cholesterol. He needs to know if your goal is to build muscle. Knowing these things will help him come up with a workout program that will fit you specifically.

After he comes up with a program, your trainer will be with you every step of the way. He will be there when you start your workouts and show you the proper technique so you don't injure yourself and you get the maximum results from the exercise that you're doing. He will be there to spot you when you're weight lifting if you're at the end of your reps and your muscles have turned to jelly and you need help getting the weights safely back on the racks. He will be focused 100% on you and your needs for your entire training session. He won't get distracted. He won't turn away. He will always be there to assist and cheer you on when necessary. He will encourage you and remind you of your end goal and the progress that you are making towards achieving that goal. Your trainer will be committed to you and to helping you achieve your goal.

Heavenly Father is like our very own loving personal trainer and this life is the gym. He knows each of us individually. He has a complete understanding of our hearts, our goals, our strengths, our weaknesses and the areas in which we need to grow. He has a personal training plan for each one of us. He has tailor-made it especially for us. There is no other person on the planet that has a training plan just like ours. Every challenge we face and trial we go through is designed to help us individually grow in the areas that we need to grow in. This life is designed to stretch and build us so that we will become celestial beings and be prepared to live with him again. This is true for everyone. Sometimes we may get frustrated that our challenges seem so heavy and difficult. Mental illness is a very heavy and difficult burden. If we have the wrong perspective, we won't learn and grow with the things Heavenly Father is trying to teach us. We will become aggravated with the process and may forget that he is there to help. We can become crushed by this heavy weight. Stick with the personal trainer.

Don't become angry with Heavenly Father for giving you a training plan that challenges you more than what you think you can do. Don't blame him for giving you a very difficult training plan. Don't become bitter and enraged over the magnitude of mental illness. Look at this as an opportunity for growth. Understand that this can be one of the greatest learning experiences of your life. I look back at all I have learned and the ways I have grown through this challenge of living with mental illness and I am grateful. I am grateful because I am a better mother, a better wife, a better friend, a better person. I am better because of mental illness.

Can you imagine if you were to go into that gym with your personal trainer and then spend the whole time complaining that the weights were heavy or that you were uncomfortable? Can you imagine becoming belligerent with your trainer because of the hard things that he was requiring of you? If you were to act like that then why in the world did you go to the gym? A gym is designed to make you uncomfortable and to build your muscles and fitness level. That is the reason you go to a gym, to get stronger. That same thing is true for this life. Growing and progressing is the reason that we're here. That's why we came to earth. That's the whole purpose for our lifetime. We can change our perspective on challenges and understand that they are not meant to be punishments or simply a nuisance until we can get them behind us. If we can look at them as opportunities for growth our entire attitude will be one that is grateful that Heavenly Father cares enough to teach us.

When I was in high school, I ran track. I did the hurdles. I have banged up knees and cool scars to prove it. I never missed practice even on the days when I really REALLY didn't feel like going. I went when it was raining. I went when I was tired. I went when I had a lot of homework. I was committed to running. As a result, my coach spent a lot of one-on-one time with me. He pushed me much harder than he did my other teammates. He critiqued and pushed and pushed some more. He addressed every aspect of my race from my start off the blocks to my running form to the number of steps I took between the hurdles all the way through to the body position across the finish line. There was nothing we didn't work on. Sometimes I wondered why he couldn't just leave me be and go badger someone else. (I even had loud sighs and grumbling going on inside my head). There were plenty of other kids on the team and he was not anywhere near as demanding with them. As the season went on I had a tremendous amount of success. I broke a twenty year old school record for the 110 meter hurdles. I won race after race. After seeing all of my success, I realized something: Coach spent time with me because he knew I was committed. He saw my potential and wanted to help me become the very best athlete I could. He knew I would do whatever it took. I noticed that some of my friends on the team were not seeing much improvement in their times as the season went on. I also noticed that Coach didn't spend much time with them even though they were there most of the time. I noticed that these friends would sometimes only give half effort. They would cut the drills short or run hill sprints at 60%. They would leave early and slack off when practice got hard. I realized that coaches work where they see hard work and potential. If the coach stops working with you, it's because he doesn't think you can improve. As an athlete, that is a bad place to be. We need coaches. They have experience. They can help us succeed. You want them to be invested enough in you to help you reach your potential.

My coach knew where I needed to go. He knew what it took to get to an elite level. He knew how to train me to become the best athlete I could. All I had to do was listen. I had to submit my will to his. I had to be willing to do whatever he asked and trust him that he knew what he was doing. If I didn't have the humility to listen to my coach and change what he was asking me to change, there would be no sense in having him coach me. I would never succeed and reach my potential as an athlete.

Heavenly Father is our perfect coach. He loves us too much and can see too much potential to let us sit on the sidelines and not grow. He gives us many opportunities as life goes on to improve. He will never give up on us. The only thing we need to do is show up and be ready to work. When the challenges come, don't sit back and complain that they're difficult. Of course it's difficult, this is a gym. Don't blame Heavenly Father for difficulties. He is our trainer and coach and it is his job to push us in areas that we are weak in even if we don't recognize it. He is patient and loving and kind. He delights in our progress. Mental illness is hard. The weights are extreme and the burdens are heavy. If there was a way for me to grow in all the ways I've grown without mental illness, I would definitely choose that route. But that is not how life works. The only way we learn lessons and grow individually is by going through really hard things. I can see the lessons that I've learned and the person I'm becoming. I would not have the compassion and sensitivity if I had not dealt with mental illness. So I wouldn't change it. I would not change the relationship I have with my Savior and the love I feel from him. I would not change my rich and meaningful life that I have because I've learned to prioritize what are absolutely the most important things for me. I wouldn't change the relationships I have in my family because of the time and energy I put into them. I learned all of these things because of mental illness. I've learned these lessons on a much deeper level than I ever would have without it. So instead of hating the process, understand that it's for a purpose. Ask yourself "Self, what can

I learn from this? How will it shape me to become a better person?"

Changing how I view trials, and this trial in particular, has relieved a lot of stress, guilt and sorrow. I can see the tremendous progress that I've made. Weights that in the beginning nearly crushed me, I now can handle with relative ease by comparison. I can see where I've grown. That vision gives me the strength to move forward knowing if I put the effort in, I will continue to get stronger and this burden will become lighter to me.

Just like training in the gym, building muscle and gaining strength doesn't happen overnight. It doesn't come from one super workout. Getting stronger comes with small, consistent daily effort that turns into habits that carry you through your life. Those strengthening habits are the keys to your success. Every step you take and every lesson you learn makes you stronger. It makes you into a better person. It helps you to develop into the person that Heavenly Father is wanting you to become. Don't be discouraged with the setbacks. Don't be discouraged if you don't feel like you're progressing. Understand that learning to thrive, not just survive with mental illness will take time. You're not going to go from rock bottom to thriving in a week. It has taken me years to grow into the person I've become. It's taken years to understand how to first manage mental illness then recognize the areas I can control that help me to thrive even with this heavy weight. I wish that I had all of this information in the beginning. I wish I had understood the medication process, how to chart and how to work with doctors and other professionals. I wish I had understood the basics and how to manage my energy budget and sort through my distorted thinking. I think if I had known these things in the beginning, it would not have taken me years to be able to thrive. I hope that by sharing this information with you, you can learn to thrive earlier. I didn't have anyone telling me the secrets of success. I didn't have anyone telling me it could be done. I didn't know anyone with mental illness that was honestly, truly happy and fulfilled in their life. I hope that you feel encouraged and hopeful about your future. I hope that you can see ways that your life will be better because of this. I hope that you believe it won't always be so hard. Just relax and be patient with the process.

This is one of the things I wish someone would have told me in the beginning. It does get better. It gets better because you get stronger. You are not a boat completely adrift in the ocean going only where the wind blows. Feeling that out of control in your life is a scary thing. You are actually steering the ship. You may not be able to control how big the waves are or what storms come through or how fast you're moving, but you can control the direction you're headed. It helps you remember that this isn't pointless suffering. This is making you strong. This is building your testimony. This is stretching your character and making your foundation solid and lasting. This is solidifying your relationship with Heavenly Father because you know that without him you are nothing but with him, you can accomplish anything. You can even thrive with mental illness.

I think often of the scripture in 2 Nephi 2:25[17] "...men are that they might have joy." When I was down, I felt like the joy had been sucked out of my world. I didn't see how living with mental illness could ever bring me joy. In hindsight (which is always 20/20 of course) I can see how much more meaningful my relationships have become. I can see the strength of my marriage as Adam and I have been through deep and difficult trials together. I can see the relationships I have with my kids and the priority that I place on them in my life. I can see that these things have brought me lasting joy and fulfillment. The path I took to get here isn't the one I imagined but I would not change my life for anything. Regardless of how I got here though, I have joy. I have real lasting joy. To quote one of the greatest movies of all time (Nacho Libre) "Be happy orphans." We can choose to be happy. We can choose to laugh. We can choose to grow. You may have to fake it till you make it for a while but you can do it.

The question you have to ask yourself is how bad do you want it? How much are you willing to give up to become stable? How much focused effort can you give? No one can do this for you. You are the only one who can make the changes necessary to be able to thrive in your life. It doesn't matter how much a loved one wants it for you, if you don't commit to taking the necessary steps to become educated and make changes, you will not improve. I'm not discounting here the absolute need for loved ones to be loving and supportive and for them to be on board with helping find solutions. I am

---

17   A scripture in the Book of Mormon

saying that you are still the boss of you. You are in charge. It's up to you to figure out what things you need and what things will help. You need to figure out what things are making it harder for you and work to eliminate those things. Becoming stable, especially in the beginning, is a full-time job. Treat it seriously and be committed to taking the next step. Don't get overwhelmed with everything. It's ok to take it one tiny step at a time. Even if you're only taking tiny steps, you will still get to your destination of thriving in your life. Have faith. Don't give up.

Learning to thrive with mental illness takes time. You will grow and improve every single day. Just put one foot in front of the other. Keep your head down and continue to take that next step. You will get to the point that you master this trial. You will feel happiness, joy and fulfillment again. You will be able to thrive. All you have to do is give it your best shot. Your best will be good enough. You don't have to be more than what you are. If you are patient with the process and rely on your own personal trainer, he will take you beyond what you thought was possible. Be willing to submit your will to his. Have trust in him and in yourself that you can handle this heavy weight. You will get better and stronger as you become more educated and practice moving forward. You will be able to thrive with mental illness. Don't be discouraged because of the difficulty of this challenge. Understand that this is the exercise Heavenly Father wants you to do. The things that you will learn from this will be specific to making you into the best possible person you can be. It will help the people around you to grow and develop in ways that they never could have otherwise. Heavenly

Father is training you to be a champion. This can be one of the greatest blessings in your life.

Mental illness has given me a great gift. It has given me the gift of living intentionally and on purpose. It's forced me to narrow down the things I want in my life to only my most important things and spending all of my time and energy there. My life is full and rich. It is richer than it would have been otherwise if I didn't have mental illness. I am not busy and overscheduled. Having more things in my life doesn't necessarily make it better. Sometimes more is just more. There is a difference between having a full life and having a busy life. My life is full. Happiness comes from living life exactly how you want to live it.

You can still take chances. You can still be courageous. You can still overcome fear. Start by learning to thrive with mental illness. Doing that will give you the confidence that you can handle anything. When I was twenty-eight Adam and I moved into our first little townhouse. We had moved into an established neighborhood and were some of the youngest adults in the ward. I had just had Sam, my second son, when I was called as the gospel doctrine[18] teacher. In that class we had the stake president[19], the stake patriarch[20] and the temple president.[21] I was terrified. Little by little though, I started to gain confi-

---

18   Sunday School

19   Church leader who is over an entire stake (stakes are made up of 7-14 wards or congregations)

20   Church leader who is called specifically to give patriarchal blessings. There is only one in each stake.

21   Church leader who runs the temple.

dence. With each lesson I became more comfortable and less anxious about whether or not I could handle that calling. That was a tremendous learning experience in my life. Ever since that calling, any other calling I've been asked to do seems like a piece of cake. Nothing will ever be as scary as that calling was to me. It's the same thing with hard challenges in your life. Learning to live with mental illness is a big challenge. When you realize that not only can you survive with mental illness, but thrive, you will have the confidence that you can overcome anything. Your faith will be stronger. You will realize that with God you can do all things. This will Increase your testimony. This will Increase your faith. This will help you recognize how remarkable you are as a human being. It will help you to see all your good qualities and areas that you have grown in with help from the Lord. You truly can accomplish anything.

If there's anything I want you to take away from this book it's that you do have control. You may not be able to control the fact that you have mental illness but you do have control over how much you let it dictate your life. Be proactive. Work hard. Most importantly, don't give up. When the dark days come (and they still will) do everything you can to take care of yourself. Some days taking care of yourself may mean sleeping in 'till 10:00 and canceling all of your commitments. If that's what you need, then you should do it. Understand what works for you. Become your own advocate and ask for what you need. And if you happen to find some keys to success for you, don't be shy. Pass them my way. I'm always on the lookout.

ACKNOWLEDGEMENTS

• • •

THIS BOOK WOULDN'T HAVE HAPPENED without so many people along the way. Thank you to Brittany Holt who introduced and encouraged the idea of writing long before I ever took you seriously. Thank you to Rebecca Brooke for your superior editing skills managing to take a jumble of thoughts and ideas and helping me to turn them into something neat, organized and digestable. Thank you to Ria Farkas for your amazing cover design. You somehow knew exactly what was in my head even though I didn't even know what it was. You're magic. Thank you to Bruce Barnes who always manages to make me look beautiful. You are a photographer extraordinaire. Thank you to Liz Robinson for always making sure I take time to play. You take me to my happy place. Thank you to Melanie St. Clair, Kim Ferrin, Marci Crismon and Alison Huston for your instrumental feedback and reading the book in its worst form.

Thank you to Mark Bell for your frankness and practicality when approaching problems. Your guidance and friendship have been invaluable to me Thank you to Dr. Eric Greenman for being the pivotal point in managing my medication to help me become stable. You were worth every penny (and that's a lot of pennies!). Thank you to Dr. Gary Smith for your genuine care and love as you've treated me. I look to you not only for your medical expertise but also for your heartfelt life guidance.

Thank you to my parents Doug and Rozanne Williams for teaching me that I can do hard things. Most of all thank you to Adam for so so many things. Thank you for all the hours of conversation helping me articulate exactly what I wanted to say. Thank you for manning the home front and understanding when you came home at night to no dinner and me still typing on the computer in my pajamas. Thank you for your encouragement and belief in me even when I doubted. I think you might be just a little bit crazy but I love you even more for it.

INDEX

Daily Mood Chart

	DAY	1	2	3	4	5	6	7	8	9	10	11	12	13	14	15	16	17	18	19	20	21	22	23	24	25	26	27	28	29	30	31
NORMAL	+3																															
	+2																															
	+1																															
LOW MOOD	-1																															
	-2																															
	-3																															

WEIGHT ON DAY 14 & 28

| ANXIETY | | | | | | 1 | | 1 | | | | 1 | 2 | 1 | | | | | | | 2 | 1 | | | | | | | | | | |
| IRRITABILITY | | 1 | | | | | | | | | | 3 | 2 | 1 | | | | | | | 1 | | | | | | | | | | |

O = quiz & cycle

MEDICATION (name/mg)

Place a checkmark if medication was taken each day

| Exercise | | | | | | | | | | | | | | | | | | | | | | | | | | | | | | | |
| | B1H | | N1Y | | W1B1H | | | X1G1H | | | | | N | B1W | | 8 | | X1G1W | | 4 | |

Name _Mequelli_   Month/Year __May__